Design and Art: Louis Wilsenach
Photographers: **Rowan Wilkinson**,
Paulo Toureiro, Natalie Baxter, Antonia De Luca
Design and Layout: Naomi Bezuidenhout
Editor: Naomi Bezuidenhout
Copy writer: Annette Nel

Recipes from Our Organic Garden
All rights reserved
Third Edition © 2013 Antonia De Luca
ISBN 978-0620-5813-2-5
Published by: God-Idea Productions
info.godideas@gmail.com
www.godideas.co.za

Special thanks to my friends, family and members of staff for their contributions to this recipe book.
Thank you for all the help, creativity and unconditional love that has made this book possible.

Louise De Luca, Gage Williams, Kotze Ellis, Bruno Reolon, Theresa Alexander, Michele and Bruce
Throssell, Petros Ngema, Yota Carle, Elizma Ruthven, Nicolas Torrent, Matthew Kenney, Peter and
Beryn Daniel, Ma, Mary-Ann Shearer, Lello Incendiario, Lesley Groenewald, Cathrine, Essie, Serna
Kramer, Ingrid Litman, Karien Steyn, Laura Smuts, Rob Harrewyn, David Avocado Wolfe, Ishvara Dhyan,
Louise Kruger, Kristeen Simonsen, Linah Mahlangu, Roland Prukl and Lee Potgieter.

This book is dedicated to my incredible, unselfish and ever-loving father.
Without him, Leafy Greens and anything that I have ever achieved,
would not have been possible.
I am so grateful. I love you with all my heart!

My name is Antonia De Luca; I am the owner and founder of Leafy Greens Café in Johannesburg, South Africa. I was born on an organic farm which is where my café is situated. I have lived on the property for most of my life.

I attended Stellenbosch University and Bond University on the Gold Coast of Australia where I completed degrees in marketing, entrepreneurship and an MBA in Finance. I have always been involved in the family business, Casalinga Restaurant, so naturally I was destined to end up in the hospitality industry, but with a difference. Being brought up a vegetarian, I opened Leafy Greens Café in June 2010, a raw food and vegan-friendly restaurant. I was inspired after travelling the USA extensively and studying nutrition and health. I completed the Life Change Program at Hippocrates Health Institute in Florida. I trained as a raw food chef under Matthew Kenney in Oklahoma and visited many raw food restaurants for inspiration, from this, my café was born!

I am delighted to present you with our recipe book.
Many long, hard hours have been put into this book.
I hope you enjoy it!
A book of healthy, handcrafted dishes from our kitchen with
ingredients from our organic garden.
Fueled by Leafy Greens.
Eat Well, Do Good!

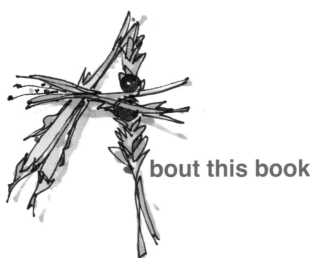

bout this book

There are two things that Italians are world-famous for – passion and wonderful food. Having grown up in a family with a passion for cooking, I have learnt a lot about Italian cuisine.

My dad encouraged me from an early age to learn and absorb all the old family recipes and traditions from my grandmother. She's shown me that cooking goes far beyond mastering the techniques – she's taught me the value of fresh ingredients and together, we have spent countless hours in the kitchen and in her garden. I have learnt the importance of quality ingredients – the sheer delight of sun-ripened ox-heart heirloom tomatoes, fragrant fresh basil and crusty home baked-breads, to name but a few.

I remember that as a young girl, I never felt right eating butter - I would visit my friends and ask for sandwiches without it. We weren't big meat eaters either, and having our own home-grown vegetables, we got most of our calories from the garden – freshly picked. It was my naturally healthy appetite, together with everything I have learnt from my grandmother, which inspired me to open Leafy Greens. The concept behind my restaurant is very unique - we design our menu around what we have in our garden – a concept that forces us to be very creative with our dishes. From the first day that Leafy Greens opened its doors, my customers have been asking for a recipe book. And now it's in your hands – your own taste of Leafy Greens. I also wrote this book because I believe it's the ideal way to preserve my grandmother's food legacy – something which is truly worth treasuring.

I hope this book will bring its readers back to life, back to eating living foods. I want people to rediscover the joy of getting back to basics. To eat simply again. To grow our own food, or at least know where our food comes from. This is taking the power back into our own hands. To savour the beauty of each fruit and vegetable. To bring the authentic flavours of vegetables, fruits and herbs to their fullness and enjoy them for health and longevity.

Thank you for being a part of my dream.

Antonia

Contents

Follow my leader

I suppose I was fortunate that I was born healthy. I also come from a family where the luxury of too much "fancy" food was not available. Good water, fresh air, exercise, sufficient sleep and a simple diet with lots of vegetables was imperative.

Gradually, through the years of my adult life, I came to realise the importance of diet. I have always stayed as far away from medication as possible, rather choosing the natural way. My wife Vivienne and I have also been most fortunate that our eldest daughter, Jennifer (Antonia's mother), became a vegetarian, then a vegan and then a raw foodist many years ago. It has been because of her positive influence that we are extremely careful of what we eat. We are also careful in our home regarding the use of soaps, cleaning materials and microwave ovens. Every day there is more evidence showing the bad effects of all these products on our health.

As our family of six children expanded to include 22 grandchildren, I have felt more than ever the need to encourage them to eat correctly, exercise and choose what is right. Be happy, be kind, and give of yourself, always. Only when you are in the service of your fellow man, are you truly in the service of your God. My faith plays a huge part in my life. It is the foundation of everything that we hold dear – love, peace, joy and spirituality. It's the light that guides me, every day.

I have travelled more than 15 million miles over these past sixty years and I will continue to do so. I could not have kept up this pace without my healthy lifestyle. I am deeply grateful to the people who have helped me on the way.

Antonia Alexandra De Luca is our eldest grandchild. We are enormously proud of her for a multitude of reasons. She has so many outstanding attributes; it is tough to know where to start. Suffice it to say, she is smart, hardworking and very beautiful. Her passion is raw food! Her restaurant, "Leafy Greens", has taken off and is very successful. If you haven't been there, you must go!

We love you, darling granddaughter.
Grandpa,

Gary Player

The Player Story...

Gary and Vivienne's wedding day.

The first time my grandpa Gary laid eyes on Vivienne, my grandmother, he said to his friend, "You see that girl - I'm going to marry her one day." No truer words have ever been spoken. But it was only after many years of practice and a win the Ampol Tournament, that my grandparents finally walked down the isle in January 1957. There is a very famous picture of my gran jumping into the air when she received the telegram from Australia saying that he had won and that they finally had enough money to get married.

Through the years, their love grew from strength to strength – and so did their family. Gary and Vivienne became the proud parents of two sons and four daughters, and all of them have become successful in their own right.

My mom, Jennifer, the first-born, is a thriving entrepreneur and an avid health fanatic. My parents, siblings and I still live on Rocky Ridge Farm in Johannesburg.

Marc, the second-born, is a businessman and marketing genius. He is married to Claudia and the proud father of three amazingly handsome and sporty boys.

The third heir to the throne is Wayne – he inherited my grandfather's golf genes. Apart from his career as a professional coach and all-round golf professional, he is a loving husband and father of three. Wayne still has the same rippling 6-pack now that he did 30 years ago.

Michele is a world-renowned interior decorator based in Durban, South Africa. She is married to Bruce Throssell and they have four beautiful children.

Theresa, a former professional dancer, model and trained French gourmet chef, lives with her husband, Des Alexander, in Cape Town. They have two lovely children.

Amanda might be the youngest, but she's the Iron Woman of the family . . . literally. She and her husband, Matthew Hall have 7 children, which fill up their Philadelphia home in the USA.

I am the eldest of 22 grandchildren and I'm proud to be part of a family of go-getters and hard workers. All born in South Africa but scattered all over the world, we're inspired by fitness, health and wholesome food and we are passionate about family.

Growing up in The Player household: Aunt Theresa remembers . . .

Sunday family lunches were sacred. Sunday roasts were the order of the day. Wayne consumed a whole chicken and who knows how many roast potatoes, all smothered in a jug of gravy, at one sitting. We had to eat all our vegetables so I always hid my peas under my gem squash. (Don't tell my mother, but to this day, I still hate peas.) In essence, the Players were a family who enjoyed large amounts of fruit, vegetables, with a vanilla ice cream and hot chocolate sauce occasionally.

Jenny with dad Gary and mom Vivienne on a beach in the Bahamas.

I remember Jenny's wild parties, and how we used to pass copious amounts of hotdogs through the kitchen window to every stranger in Honeydew, being promised 5 cents if they could phone Michele when she turned 21. I also recall how Marc used to chase Wayne around the kitchen table with a carving knife, after he had demolished all the tuna mayo. And I remember that everything in the household was homemade. The smell of delicious aromas of Mama Essie's homemade whole-wheat bread and date muffins baking in the oven and I can still see her beautiful chocolate skin, cool eyes and warm disposition.

Those were the days . . . the days of riding our horses bareback on the farm, picking strawberries in our garden and getting mud on our clothes in pure childhood bliss. I remember the misty mornings, the sound of rain on the tin roof and grandpa yodelling. I remember fishing, foofy slides, windswept hair from sitting on the back of the bakkie, and singing like a rhinestone cowboy! And how could I ever forget 'Boy named Sue!' and how Wayne stood on the dinner table entertaining everybody, because he knew every word.

Those were good days. Unforgettable days. And I feel privileged to have grown up in the Player family. A family that overcame its tough beginnings to really bloom in every single way.

Fitness fanatics from day one.

This is a "Marriage—and £5,000" Jump for Joy: and it's the Year's HAPPIEST Picture

"Sunday Times" Reporter

VEREENIGING, Saturday. — "The happiest girl in South Africa" was how 19-year-old, brunette Vivienne Verwey, described herself at the Maccauvlei golf course, across the Vaal River from Vereeniging, to-day.

The reason: Young (21) Gary Player, her fiancé and South Africa's "successor to Bobby Locke", had won the £5,000 first prize in the Ampol golf tournament at Yarra Yarra, Australia. And before he won he declared: "If I win. I will marry Vivienne immediately."

Vivienne told me: "This is the sort of thing one dreams about but never quite believes will happen. Gary has been playing superb golf lately. Call it a woman's intuition if you like, but I had a strange feeling that he would win."

Go Overseas With Him

Final plans for the wedding would be made when Gary Player arrived home early in December, she said.

(Meanwhile a cable from Gary was on its way to her reading: "We've won £5,000 and will marry immediately.")

"But nothing can be decided then — I can only say that the wedding will be before the South African Open in April.

"After that Gary will make for England, where he will compete in the British Open. When the time comes, he will make a bid for the Tam 'O Shanter tournament in America."

Vivienne is determined to accompany Gary Player on his next overseas trip. She will not be left behind so soon after the marriage, she said.

An outstanding golfer in own right, she will be able to hold her own in any company if she does go overseas.

Mrs. Verwey, Vivienne's mother, was also at Maccauvlei, where 15-year-old Bobby, her son and the newest South African golfing prodigy, was competing in a tournament.

"I know they will be very happy." she said.

Earlier, Bobby had been defeated two and one by the burly, long-hitting Peter Vorster (Bloemfontein) in the Maccauvlei tournament.

Nineteen-year-old Vivienne Verwey jumps with joy at the Maccauvlei golf course, Vereeniging, yesterday, when she hears that her fiance, Gary Player, had won the £5,000 Ampol golf tournament in Melbourne, Australia. Before the match Gary declared: "If I win, I will marry Vivienne

This picture, taken as Vivienne received news of Gary's victory that ensured they were financially able to marry, received an award for news photograph of the year.

Famous picture of my grandmother jumping for joy when she received the telegraph from Australia, stating that my Grandpa had won the Ampol Tournament.

13

The De Luca Story

Aldo and Marguerite De Luca on their wedding day

To the world she was Marguerite De Luca. To us, she was just plain Ma. Yet there was nothing "just plain" about my mother.

Born in 1930 in Cheltondale, Johannesburg, this formidable woman knew the meaning of hard work, and she certainly didn't mind getting her hands dirty.

At her father's garage, she helped with petrol pump readings and to fix the trucks. It was here, with rolled up sleeves and grease on her hands, that she fell in love with a co-worker – my father. Ma and Aldo De Luca got married very young - maybe too young. Life for them was tough. Aldo was always working and my mother had to bring up the four of us, all by herself. One of the lowest points for the family, was when Aldo left Ma. He wasn't very involved in our lives and life was far from easy.

After their divorce, Ma moved to Random Harvest in Muldersdrift – her heart's home – the farm she still works and loves today. Back then, the property was completely overgrown and dilapidated. It was here, while trying to build something from nothing, that she rediscovered her passion and vigour for life. She loved the earth, and the earth loved her – the days upon days that she spent working the soil, rewarded her with baskets that were overflowing with an abundance of plump crops. I can still vividly remember the stone-ground polenta that she made from the corn that she grew. There were hearty brown beans, traditional Italian cabbage dishes, and of course crisp, dew-fresh salads – all grown in her very own piece of Eden.

My sister, Linda, started Random Harvest Indigenous Nursery on that same farm, and it is still in operation today. Just like Ma, Linda is also a hands-on worker. Hard work is clearly a family trait, because my other sister, Louise, is the same - she has a love for horses and, boy, does this woman know how to cook. Antonia's first introduction to whipping up culinary delights in Louise's kitchen, was battered zucchini. She would pick the baby marrows from the garden, wash and slice them paper-thin on Louise's mandolin. Louise showed Antonia how to prepare the bowl with eggs and flour before dipping the zucchini in the batter and pan-frying them. Antonia learned this before she learned how to peel a mango.

Aunt Louise and Antonia

After many years and countless calluses, Ma built a life for her family on the farm. A life with many ups and downs, but lots of fond memories for everybody. Everything she did, was for her family. Except the tennis court – this was a self-indulgence that she saved up for over a very long time. Ma loved tennis. But shortly after her tennis-court dream became a reality, she injured her leg in a terrible tractor accident, and the court just served as a cruel reminder of the fact that she would never be able to play tennis again.

Her hard work and passion are showcased in the bounty of her laden pantry shelves. There's nothing you can teach this woman about preserving, pickling and bottling. Ma is an incredible cook who has mastered these techniques and who knows how to never let anything go to waste. I have fond memories of eating preserved peaches, fresh mulberries and homemade jams at Ma's house as a kid. I would open her freezer and everything was perfectly packed. Her almost prehistoric Tupperware containers were always in mint condition. She is just as good at taking care of her things as she is of taking care of us. She helped Jenny and me to develop the original menu at Casalinga. She trained all of our staff too. Even to this day, Ma still actively helps our family with just about anything. We call her "Mrs. Fixit" – because whether it's a tractor or a jersey, she knows how to repair it. In fact, she is just as comfortable with a pair of knitting needles as she is with a pair of pliers.

And then there was my dad, Aldo De Luca. This diligent man was born to Filomena and Guilio De Luca in the little town Lucca, in Tuscany.

His family was struggling to make a living in Italy due to the war and decided to look for a better life in South Africa. My dad grew up in Kew on a vegetable farm where he took care of the chickens, rabbits, cows and vegetables. He was a real farm-boy and always told us how he used to squirt raw goats milk straight into his mouth.

Growing up was simple, but hard. His family picked vegetables until the early hours of the morning so that they could be delivered to market, freshly picked, a few hours later. My dad had to walk miles to deliver the milk to neighbours and customers, but walking was something Aldo was used to – after all, he had to walk 12km to school every day. And he did most of this route with his shoes in his hands, just to make sure they didn't wear out too quickly. In 1933, during the Great Depression, things were really tough, but the food from their own land was their saving grace.

Aldo never shied away from hard work. He traded in old petrol trucks, and slowly but surely saved up enough money to start his own business in 1955: Pauls Sand. He kept his head down and went on to start four other successful businesses. His last venture was at age 74 – Al Fresco Restaurant, just up the road from Leafy Greens. Somehow, food has always been a part of our lives.

Interesting entry on Peter's grandmother Adelaide's passport: under professione; 'Casalinga', housewife, which was our inspiration for our restaurant.

With Aldo working so close to our home, our family got much closer to him in his golden years. He always had an interesting story to tell and his positivity was contagious. He treated his staff with the utmost respect and we will always remember him for his great sense of humour.

Aldo passed away in 2008. We miss him, every day.

Peter De Luca

Aldo, Peter's dad, with his dog and his vegetable garden in the background.

Rocky Ridge Farm

For as long as I remember, I've always been a hands-on kind of guy. I did a technical matric, went to Art College and did an apprenticeship as a joiner and cabinet maker. While I was at college, I worked in restaurants at night to pay for my studies. For years I wore the La Lampara Restaurant apron in Norwood, where I worked for my good friend, Pino Canderle.

But this famous restaurant wasn't my first encounter with my love for food . . .

I vividly remember my Nona and the incredible recipes that she whipped up when we were kids. One particular dish that stands out in my mind, was one-day-old bread served with coffee and sugar in a bowl for breakfast. Nona was from Piedmont in Italy and everybody who came from that area was poor, so my family always knew how to live off the land. She made rabbit in batter, and a cabbage bake that was layered with bread and smothered with cheese. Our food was mostly vegetable based. It was hearty food. Soul food.

My mother and my Nona taught me about organic gardening and the art of picking the vegetables correctly to ensure the best possible crops. Nostalgic memories of the bountiful fig trees, walking between the beanstalks, running in the water canals, fresh melanzane (eggplant), zucchini and fagioli (beans) have kept my passion for organic gardening alive through the decades. On her farm in Muldersdrift, my mother bottled and preserved everything that she reaped, made her own butter and cream and milked her own cows. She must be one of the most capable women on the planet. If you want something done, give it to my mother - gardening, seed saving, bottling, preserving, sewing, cooking . . . you name it. She is a Jane of All Trades, master of all. She has always been one of my greatest inspirations and taught me the value of natural food and healthy living. We have indeed always been good-food-people.

So when I left college, my wife Jennifer and I naturally went straight into the food business – while our peers were thinking of painting the town red, the 21-year-old Jenny and I were thinking of fresh juices. We opened the Big Squeeze Juice Bar and served freshly extracted melon, orange, fruit cocktail, naartjie and grapefruit juice. We also baked our own bread and served the most delectable whole-wheat sandwiches. People came from far and near to dig into our homemade pies and, of course, our frozen bananas dipped in chocolate. My sister, Louise, made our fresh yogurt.

After just a year, we sold the Big Squeeze and made a sizable profit.

We then took our passion for serving to Louis Trichard, where we bought the first traditional African restaurant in this conservative town. Our focus on great service and mouthwatering food quickly made us very popular among the local community. We then sold this business and moved back to Johannesburg to join the Adamo family in the Cortina Restaurant in Hyde Park. Here I was tossing pizza dough and rolling out fresh pasta for the Cortina Pasta takeaway outlet attached to the restaurant. I loved kneading and cooking and the exciting buzz of the kitchen. I learned many valuable lessons from the Cortina boys, especially Ida and Carlo Adamo. At that point, they were the best Italian restaurateurs in town.

At about the same time, I started a golf driving range and a vegetable garden on my farm in Muldersdrift. My family always grew vegetables at home – a healthy tradition I was adamant to continue. I had a golf shack at Rocky Ridge Farm where I served cheesecake, carrot cake and coffee. (We got a fabulous cheesecake recipe from my cousin Simone Nucci - she was a superb dessert chef.) The food in our shack became very popular and guests at my driving range started prodding me about opening a restaurant. This request wasn't new - Jenny and I entertained a lot at home and our friends have always encouraged us to open a restaurant. So we did. We called it Casalinga, meaning 'housewife' or 'homemade.'

When Jenny and I decided to open the restaurant, it took us ages to get the finance - our fathers were tough and we had to come up with the money ourselves. We eventually got a loan from Bank of Lisbon, whom we are still loyal till today.

I designed and built the restaurant myself. It was completely sustainable - we bought only secondhand materials and used bricks from demolished mining houses. The windows and doors were secondhand too. Casalinga had a local, rustic and homely décor and ambiance, so it just worked. My mother, Marguerite De Luca, helped us with our menus, recipes and she taught our chefs to make pasta, gnocchi, and other traditional Italian dishes. We also began expanding the vegetable garden to supply Casalinga with fresh produce – we wanted to serve food directly from the earth to the table.

Casalinga is more than a restaurant. It's sharing something we love with the world at a place that's an extension of our home. As Casalinga grew, the hours grew longer and the work became more strenuous. I needed energy – so I dosed up on coffee, drank whiskey and surrendered myself to cigarettes, just to stay awake and motivated. We ate a lot too – we tasted everything. We ate on the go and we were eating way too many refined carbohydrates. My energy levels and my health took a turn for the worse and I developed an ulcer and psoriasis. I eventually decided to knock on the door of Mary-Ann Shearer from The Natural Way and she helped me to change my lifestyle through fasting, eating raw food and juicing. My first fast was 18 days on water alone. I felt absolutely fantastic - I felt completely rested, I lost weight and healed my ulcer.

It was at this point that I decided to become vegetarian, followed by veganism and later on, mainly a raw food diet. I stopped drinking and smoking and I instantly felt better, healthier and lighter. Then I fasted again with Dr. Charlotte Prout Jones at the Life Science Clinic in Johannesburg. I learned a lot about raw food, colon health and cleansing from Charlotte.

In 2010, I visited Hippocrates Health Institute in Palm Beach, Florida, USA. Here I cleansed for 2 weeks under the guidance of Dr. Brian Clement. I learned about wheatgrass, sprouting, enemas, pure water and green juices. It was a real eye-opener – a new awareness and awe for my body and what makes it tick, and learning about the main causes of disease.

A few months later, my daughter, Antonia, came up with the fantastic idea of opening Leafy Greens. I supported her, and together, we realised her dream when we opened its doors in June 2010. Just like Casalinga, Leafy Greens is an extension of our home, where we'll always welcome our customers with true Italian hospitality and passion. We hope that you will taste the love in the home-grown, handcrafted food on offer on our farm.

But Leafy Greens is just part of my journey. A journey to a better life. A journey that I continue to walk, every day. My current focus is on my spiritual life, the Art of Living, love and compassion through meditation and stilling the mind.

Our family's path has been an interesting one. I am grateful for my health, my family and my business. I wish my daughter the greatest of luck with this book. May this inspire many readers to plant their own garden and to live an abundant life, naturally.

Peter De Luca

Inspiration...

My love affair with food began when I was just three months old and my mom introduced me to porridge with full cream milk. I have Nanny Maples to thank for this, as she was the one who told my mom that her breast milk was insufficient for me. I didn't like food – I loved food. And this growing passion soon led to a growing number of fat cells.

Although my love for food hasn't changed, I have changed course and direction and today I eat a predominantly raw food diet rich in sprouts, herbs, green vegetable juice, wheatgrass and, on occasion, some cooked organic vegetables.

But I wasn't always this healthy. When we started Casalinga in 1989, we opened ourselves up to many long, hard hours and a lot of stressful nights. Soon, I found myself eating and drinking four nights a week and partying more than my body could handle. My husband, Peter, who had developed an ulcer from stress and living on whiskey and pasta, met Mary-Ann and Mark Shearer in the restaurant. We soon became very close friends and through their treasured mentorship, Mary-Ann helped us both to go 'The Natural Way.' Exercise also became an integral part of my life.

My extra pounds quickly melted away and through fasting, Peter's ulcer disappeared too. We felt a new lease on life. We drank less, gave up coffee and slowly adopted a vegetarian lifestyle. I have to confess that, for me, bread and cheese were the hardest to give up. But after a seven year long journey, I've accomplished this. The fact that I progressively became healthier and felt better helped the cause tremendously. I've never looked back.

In 2009, I met Peter and Beryn Daniel from Superfoods and Rawlicious and went 'raw 'for about two years. During this time, I went on a trip to India for four weeks and managed on a raw food diet. This trip definitely didn't go without its challenges - the quality of raw foods and salads were very poor. To this day, I still pop some avocado and sprouts in my bag when eating out. Just in case.

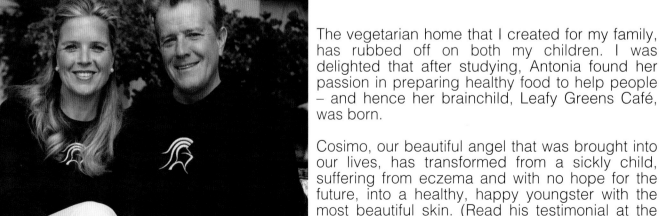

The vegetarian home that I created for my family, has rubbed off on both my children. I was delighted that after studying, Antonia found her passion in preparing healthy food to help people – and hence her brainchild, Leafy Greens Café, was born.

Cosimo, our beautiful angel that was brought into our lives, has transformed from a sickly child, suffering from eczema and with no hope for the future, into a healthy, happy youngster with the most beautiful skin. (Read his testimonial at the back of this book.)

Gary and Jennifer

When we started eating like this it was purely for our health, but it soon became a conscious effort to start living sustainably. We grow our own vegetables and we make every effort to help our ailing planet and to prevent cruelty to animals. The way people treat them, is inhumane. As consumers, and I include myself here, we are often oblivious to the cruelty and animal testing involved in making a pretty lipstick.

I went to Hippocrates Health Institute in 2010 to learn and discover more about health. Hippocrates specialises in helping people with cancer by going the natural way. Here I saw the sweetest miracles happening every day, which is why I decided to go back to do the nine-week health educator program in 2013.

I believe all the answers we need could be found in nature, but sadly mankind has been led so far astray that we have forgotten about balance in life. From a very early age our youths are pushed into the stress and pressures of a fast and busy schedule. People work too hard, play too hard, strive only for money and then, when their health goes, use all their money to rely on doctors to make them better. It just doesn't make sense.

I believe that we need to live in a state of perpetual inspiration – there is so much out there to be inspired by and enchanted about. We hope you enjoy this book and find your magic.

Eat Well, Do Good!
Jenny De Luca

My Passion

My parents founded Casalinga, their Italian restaurant, in 1989. They poured their hearts and souls into the place and worked hard at it, day in and night out, with blood sweat and tears. In fact, my parents never went on holiday together for the first eight years of the business, as one of them always had to be at the restaurant. But eventually their lifestyle caught up with them – too many late nights and too much eating and drinking finally took its toll on their health. Something had to change, drastically. They started juicing, mainly carrots, but this was the beginning of our consciousness of what we put into our bodies. At the same time, my mother started educating herself about healthy living. She devoured any book or article she could lay her hands on to learn about things like raw food, vegetarianism, colon health, cancer prevention and eating for longevity.

Fortunately, being Italian, we always ate seasonal food from our organic garden, we had a natural love for fruits and vegetables and we knew how to prepare them well. This was a great help with our transition to a vegetarian diet. We have been blessed to have wonderful vegetable gardens on our farm. My grandmother passed many of her heritage seeds on to my father, who has turned growing vegetables into a very successful operation. The organic garden on our farm produced bountiful crops of artichokes, kale, spinach, black figs, tomatoes, herbs and much more. My Italian grandmother, taught us how to preserve this beautiful produce through pickling and bottling – jars upon jars of peaches, pears, beetroots, artichokes, beans, plums, jams, chillies, spreads and tomato sauces have always filled the pantry shelves, thanks to her expert hands. In turn, I have developed a great love for preserving food without sugar and preservatives, using old-fashioned methods.

Our family has always been inspired by food – from the way it grows and the seeds it came from to the soil it grows in and the unique taste of each and every vegetable. Even with having Casalinga Restaurant for many years, we have always focused on fruits and vegetables and how we could make proper use of what we grew here on Rocky Ridge Farm. We love organic produce! This was part of the inspiration behind Leafy Greens... People have long forgotten what vegetables really taste like. They have forgotten the flavour of a dark red ripe tomato, hand-grown and handpicked from the vine. There is a real joy in knowing where your food comes from, and by growing some of it yourself, we make a decision to put our health first and to be more conscious eaters. After all, we should all be able to choose the farmer who raises or grows our food. We should have the right to speak to him and hear about his methods. We should have a right to know the mineral content of his soil and whether or not his seeds are genetically modified. We should be able to see the fertilizers, pesticides and steroids that he uses and decide whether we are willing to partake of them or not.

When we eat from the earth, we are feeding at the bottom of the food chain. This allows us to eliminate a lot of diseases, worms, bacteria and viruses that would be more predominant in for example, a lion versus its grass-eating prey, the impala.

We are also able to harness more of the sun's direct energy and the minerals from the soil that our bodies so desperately need.

In addition, growing our own food is the only truly sustainable choice for the future. Food safety is not something that our governments can guarantee us. Just look at what happened in our neighbouring country, Zimbabwe – there was a time when no food was available on the supermarket shelves. It's a harsh reality. A reality that may well happen in other countries, including our own in time to come. If we have the skills to grow our own food and to save some of our own seeds, we take the power back into our own hands. Power, that comes with a lot of joy and great health.

Last but not least, getting in touch with our own food, picking it ourselves and creating our own dishes, bring an immense joy into our lives and into the lives of our children. Children are not naturally fussy eaters - if they learn to make things like smoothies, salads and juices themselves, they will most likely eat them with relish and enjoy them immensely. Getting them involved every step of the way is also the only way to change your lifestyle permanently. It's the small changes that you make, that you stick to, that truly improves your health.

I believe strongly that I received a message and a talent from God, one that I need to share with the world. Having had the opportunity to study at Hippocrates Health Institute and gaining valuable health knowledge, I felt that the best way to spread the word would be through a restaurant - people will always need to eat! Besides, I have a deep-rooted love for taking raw materials and adding value to them, to find a beautiful way of presenting them in the most mouth-watering way. In a way that would entice people to try it at least once – then they are bound to love it.

By bringing out a recipe book, I hope to take this message into even more homes. In our fast-paced world, I know that quick, easy and healthy meals are vital – moms simply don't have the time to cook fancy, time-consuming meals. That's why I have included recipes in this book that are very doable – I want them to be incorporated as much as possible into my readers' daily lives.

Let's face it, the benefits of a clean, raw, organic, home-grown diet are endless. You will feel amazing, you will naturally return to your body's ideal weight, you will enjoy great energy levels and you will have a much more positive attitude towards life in general. If I were you, I'd say, where do I sign up?

Changing the world one meal at a time.
Eat Well, Do good!

Antonia De Luca

tips for a healthy life

Start the morning with lots of water and lemon juice. This helps to cleanse and hydrate the body. It's always best to drink water on an empty stomach.

Eat only fruits or greens in the morning - the longer you go without food the better. This allows the body a few hours to fast and cleanse.

Start every meal with something raw like a green salad, a sliced tomato, cucumber or half an avocado. The raw food gets the digestive enzymes flowing which helps to digest any cooked food. Eat bigger helpings of raw food since cooked food has no enzymes left in it and thus causes illness in the body.

It is highly beneficial to eat only when the sun is shining. Eating dinner too late does not allow your food to digest fully, interfering with the quality of sleep that you get and leaves you feeling tired in the morning.

It's a good idea to take a digestive enzyme supplement and probiotic as this balances the flora in the gut and aids with digestion. Digestion is such an important process in the body as it breaks down our food allowing for assimilation of vitamins and minerals. Food that is digested well will not stay in the colon too long.

Vegetable juices are a great way to get a lot of nutrition from greens and fruits in a predigested form. The body does not have to do any work to digest juices, they can be absorbed immediately for radiant health.

Fibre is just as important as it keeps the bowels moving. Ingesting fibre in the form of smoothies and salads is a good idea.

Do not eat fried food, takeaways, microwaved meals, processed foods or fizzy drinks. Eat food that will make you beautiful inside and out. God's food straight from the earth is the best: greens, sprouts, fruits, grasses, flowers, herbs, seeds, nuts, seaweeds, superfoods, superherbs, fermented foods and vegetables.

Drink pure, clean, living water. Most tap water contains chemicals, radiation, heavy metals, pharmaceutical drugs and fluoride. These are very bad for the body and should not be consumed knowingly.

Only grass fed animal proteins should be eaten. High quality proteins should be sourced and eaten sparingly with lots of raw greens and digestive enzymes. Other sources of protein that are easier to digest include spirulina, sunflower sprouts, pea greens, micro herbs, hemp, rice, nuts and seeds and legumes.

Include healthy fats in your diet in the form of coconut oil, olive oil, olives, nuts, seeds and avocados in their raw and unheated state for a healthy heart and brain. Think about eating for longevity and choosing wisely what you put in your mouth. Food such as olive oil, raw chocolate, local raw honey, red port wine (resveratrol), contribute to a long and healthy life.

Move your body as much as possible. Activities such as running, walking, yoga, breathing, taking the stairs instead of the lift will contribute to a healthier heart and a happy body and mind.

A happy body also comes from a well-managed inner self. Take control of your emotional health. Stress and anxiety can be managed by seeking a space and time where you can quite your mind, meditate, spend time in nature, listen to the birds and live in the moment.

Vitamin D balances many processes of the body. It can be obtained from a good plant-based supplement source and from the sun in the early and late hours of the day.

Eliminate all toxins in the form of herbicides, pesticides, toxic household cleaners, toothpaste, body products, deodorants, bath products, etc.

Eat organic food wherever possible.

Fine-tune your wake sleep cycle. Ensure that you sleep in a very dark bedroom by turning off unneeded light sources and remove all electronic devices from your bedroom. Ensure that you do not sleep with your cellphone next to your head, as this is very harmful to the body.

Listen to your body.

all our recipes are 100% vegan,
with no animal products whatsoever,
just the way nature intended them to be...

Recipe Index

C = cup
T = tablespoon
t = teaspoon

Let nature be your guide

Raw Foods

We only use the highest quality
ingredients in our recipes:
extra virgin olive oil, rock salt that is non-iodized,
organic apple cider vinegar, organic tamari,
raw nuts and seeds, etc.
We use organic, local and seasonal produce
and ingredients wherever possible.
We design our menu around our garden produce
from farm to table.

Cooked Vegan

Dips & sauces

Snacks

Desserts

Fresh Juices

pre-digested, iron & protein rich
easily absorbed nutrients
in living liquid form...

Green Juice

Green Juice

Ingredients

3 kale leaves
2 spinach leaves
1 carrot
1 apple
1 lemon
½ cucumber
1 celery stalk
2 cm ginger

Optional additions:
carrot tops, sunflower sprouts, pea greens,
cabbage leaves, sorrel (perennial herb - very high in Vitamin A
& C), stinging nettle, purslane (succulent - very high in vitamin
A &E & B), etc.

Method

Juice all of these ingredients in a slow juice press.
Drink as soon as possible as the enzymes are at its
nutritional peak when freshly juiced.
Juice can last up to 2 days in the fridge.
Serves 2.

Nothing tastes as good as thin & healthy feels.

Paw Paw, Lime and Aloe Nourisher

Ingredients

¼ paw paw, medium, peeled
¼ C water
¼ C ice
1 t aloe vera leaf, peeled
½ lime, juice
1 t liquid sweetener of your choice

Method

Blend all the ingredients on high.
Serve chilled.
Lasts up to a day in the fridge.
Serves 2.

Beetle Juice

This drink is loaded with iron and other minerals.

Ingredients

½ beetroot
2 pears
¼ small pineapple
2 carrots
1 cm piece of ginger
½ C ice

Method

Juice through a slow juice press.
Serve with ice.
Lasts up to 2 days in the fridge.
Serves 2.

*The Oscar Juicers are pioneers in single auger juicing technology.
It is a very gentle process to extract juice from fruits
and vegetables. Thus the very best way to juice!
Available in store at Leafy Greens Café.*

Paw Paw, Lime and Aloe Nourisher

Beetle Juice

Raw Mint Mojito

Ingrid's Apple Sherbet

Raw Mint Mojito

Ingredients

¼ C sake or vodka
12 mint leaves, bruised
1 C ice
6 T lemon or lime juice, freshly
squeezed
4 T liquid sweetener of your choice
½ C sparkling water or soda
4 slices fresh lime

Method

Place ice, alcohol, mint, lime juice and
sweetener in a beverage shaker.
Shake well.
Serve over ice in a glass.
Top with splash of soda and garnish
with a slice of lime and mint leaf.
Lasts a day in the fridge.
Serves 2.

Ingrid's Apple Sherbet

Ingredients

3 apples, golden delicious
1 lemon, with ¼ of its skin still on

Method

Juice the ingredients through a slow
juice press.
Serve chilled with ice and mint.
Lasts up to 2 days in the fridge.
Serves 2.

Benefits of Wheatgrass

One shot of wheatgrass juice contains over 100 vitamins, minerals and amino acids. It is equal to approximately one kilogram of fresh green vegetables. It is very high in chlorophyll and vitamins A, B, C, E and K. It is a natural source of laetrile (vitamin B17), that is normally difficult to get. It contains beta-carotene, which is found in red, green and yellow foods. Beta-carotene acts as a scavenger against harmful molecules flowing naturally through the body and through toxins inhaled from smoking, air pollution and other damaging sources. It also aids in weight loss and cleansing. It protects us against carcinogens and free radicals in the body that are cancer causing.

It rebuilds the immune system.
It is a blood cleanser. It is a powerful de-toxing agent, it helps to increase enzyme levels in the body that are anti-aging. Wheatgrass builds red blood cells and oxygenates the body. It aids digestion, regenerates and stimulates the liver. Wheatgrass is good for pets too.

Wheatgrass should be consumed daily in the form of a juice. Best taken in the morning on an empty stomach for the most benefits.

It should be drunk as soon as it has been juiced as it oxidizes rapidly.

Wheatgrass Cocktail

Ingredients

1 C apple juice, fresh
½ C sparkling water
1 frozen wheatgrass ice block (juice wheatgrass and freeze in ice tray)

Method

Pour the ingredients into a glass.
Serve with the wheatgrass ice block.
Must be consumed immediately.
Does not last in the fridge.
Serves 1.

Tomato Cocktail

Lemon Cordial and Aloe Uplift

Ingredients

½ C lemon juice, fresh
1 T aloe vera leaf, peeled
2 T liquid sweetener of your choice
1½ C sparkling water

Method

Blend the ingredients on high until light and foamy. Serve chilled.
Lasts up to 2 days in the fridge.
Serves 2.

Almond Joy

Ingredients

1 ½ C almond milk
½ vanilla pod, scraped
½ t liquid sweetener of your choice
1 ½ T lemon juice
¼ C ice

Method

Blend the ingredients on high.
Serve chilled with a slice of lemon on the side.
Lasts up to a day in the fridge.
Serves 2.

Tomato Cocktail

Ingredients

3 tomatoes, medium, ripe
1 medium slice of pineapple
¼ C water
1 T ginger, juiced
1 T lemon juice, fresh
¼ C ice
Black pepper to taste
Red Tabasco to taste

Method

Blend the ingredients until smooth. Serve with black pepper on top and a dash of red Tabasco.
Lasts 1 day in the fridge.
Serves 1.

Ginger Shot

Ginger has excellent immune building properties.

Juice one large chunk of ginger. This is enough for one shot. Drink it as soon as possible in order to benefit from the enzymes.
Serve with a wedge of orange as a chaser.
Lasts 1 day in the fridge.

Smoothies

the easiest and tastiest way
to drink your superfoods, super herbs
and greens... true fast food!

Aloe Berry Smoothie

Ingredients

½ C mixed berries, frozen
1 T goji berries
1 T aloe vera leaf, peeled
2 dates, pitted
¾ C water or almond milk
1 T mesquite powder (white carob)
1 t purple corn powder
1 t maca powder
½ C ice

Method

Blend the ingredients on high until smooth. Serve chilled.
Lasts up to 2 days in the fridge.
Serves 1.

Mixed Berry Smoothie

Ingredients

1 large banana, frozen
1 ½ C mixed frozen berries
4 dates, pitted
1 T goji berries
2 T almonds, soaked for 8 hours
1 t camu camu berry powder (vitamin C)
1 t lucuma powder (antioxidant superfruit)
1 C water
½ C ice

Method

Blend the ingredients on high.
Serve chilled.
Lasts up to 2 days in the fridge.
Serves 2.

Maca is good for strength and endurance & hormone balancing

52

Mixed Berry Smoothie

Piña Colada

Piña Colada

Ingredients

1 C coconut milk, tinned
1 ½ C pineapple juice
1 C pineapple chunks, finely chopped
1 T liquid sweetener of your choice
½ C ice
¼ C water or sake (Japanese Rice Wine for an alcoholic version)

Method

Blend the ingredients, except the pineapple chunks. Pour the liquid into a glass over the chunks and stir. Garnish with pineapple or mint.
Serve chilled.
Lasts up to 2 days in the fridge.
Serves 3.

Mango Smoothie

Ingredients

1 mango, peeled
2 T cashews
1 C almond milk
2 dates, pitted
1 t maca powder
1 C ice

Method

Blend the ingredients on high.
Serve chilled.
Lasts a day in the fridge.
Serves 1.

Mango Lassi

Mango Lassi

Ingredients

1 C mango, peeled, frozen
1 C soy milk, non-GM
2 T cashews
1 T liquid sweetener of your choice
1 T lucuma powder
½ C ice

Method

Blend the ingredients on high.
Serve chilled.
Lasts up to 2 days in the fridge.
Serves 2.

Gage's Spirulina Smoothie

Ingredients

1 banana, frozen
2 kiwi fruit, peeled
½ C orange juice
¾ C apple juice
1 C coconut water
1 t spirulina powder

Method

Blend the ingredients until smooth.
Serve chilled.
Lasts up to a day in the fridge.
Serves 1.

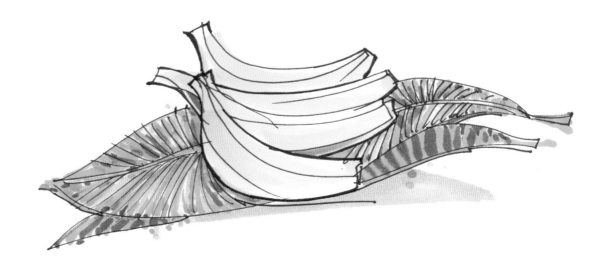

Banana Smoothie

Ingredients

2 large bananas, frozen
¾ C water or almond milk
1 t lucuma powder
1 t maca powder
2 T almonds, soaked for 1 hour
4 dates, pitted
¼ vanilla pod, scraped
½ C ice

Method

Blend the ingredients on high.
Serve chilled.
Lasts up to a day in the fridge.
Serves 2.

Banana Smoothie

Soaking almonds releases the enzyme inhibitors which makes it easier to digest. Almonds can be soaked for 1 to 24 hours.

Chocolate Smoothie

Ingredients

2 large bananas, frozen
3 T cacao powder (raw cocoa)
2 T cacao nibs
1 T maca powder
6 dates, pitted
3 T almonds, soaked for 1 hour
¾ C water or almond milk
½ C ice

Method

Blend the ingredients on high.
Serve chilled with more cacao nibs
on top.
Lasts a day in the fridge.
Serves 2.

Banana Passion

Ingredients

2 bananas, medium, frozen
1 orange, juiced
2 apples, juiced
1 t maca powder
¼ C ice

Method

Blend the ingredients on high until
smooth. Serve chilled.
Lasts 2 days in the fridge.
Serves 2.

Superfood Smoothie

Ingredients

2 large bananas, frozen
¾ C water or almond milk
2 T almonds, soaked for 1 hour
1 t lucuma powder
1 t maca powder
1 t cacao nibs
½ t spirulina powder
½ t green powder of your choice (wheatgrass, moringa, barleygrass, etc.)
1 T goji berries
1 t cinnamon powder
4 dates, pitted
½ C ice

Method

Blend the ingredients on high.
Serve chilled.
Lasts up to a day in the fridge.
Serves 2.

Thai Green Coconut Smoothie

Ingredients

1 C coconut milk
¼ C cashews
1 medium pineapple, frozen
1 C kale leaves, stems removed
2 bananas, frozen
1 T coconut oil, melted
2 dates, pitted
1 T coriander leaves, fresh
1 C ice
Pinch of salt

Method

Place all of the ingredients together in a blender and blend until smooth.
Lasts up to 2 days in the fridge.
Freezes well.
Serves 4.

Add ice towards the end for a bit of crunch.

Superfood Smoothie

Pineapple and Kiwi Cocktail

Pineapple and Kiwi Cocktail

Ingredients

1 kiwi fruit, peeled
1 C pineapple, peeled and chopped
4 mint leaves, fresh
1 t liquid sweetener of your choice
¾ C sparkling water
¼ C ice

Method

Blend the ingredients on low.
Serve chilled.
Lasts a day in the fridge.
Serves 1.

Paw Paw and Almond Milk

Ingredients

1 paw paw, peeled and chopped
1 T lemon juice, fresh
1 t liquid sweetener of your choice
¼ C almond milk
1 t cinnamon powder

Method

Blend the paw paw, lemon juice
and sweetener until smooth.
Fill a tall glass three quarters full.
Top up with the almond milk and a
sprinkle of cinnamon.
Serve chilled.
Lasts a day in the fridge.
Serves 2.

Purple Sunset

Ingredients

1 medium pineapple, fresh
2 bananas, frozen
1 C mango, diced
1 ½ C almond or coconut milk
½ vanilla pod, scraped
3 dates, pitted
Pinch of salt
1 C mixed berries

Method

Blend all the ingredients (except the berries) until smooth and pour three quarters of this mixture into a glass.
Blend the remaining mixture with the berries and fill up the glass.
Serve with some fresh berries or a dash of coconut milk on top.
Lasts a day in the fridge.
Serves 3.

Purple Sunset

Green Protein Smoothie

Ingredients

2 large bananas, frozen
¾ C water or almond milk
4 dates, pitted
½ t spirulina powder (protein, iodine)
½ t moringa powder (liver and kidney detox)
1 C organic leafy greens (kale, spinach, lettuce, etc.)
1 t maca powder
½ C ice

Method

Blend the ingredients on high.
Serve chilled.
Lasts up to 2 days in the fridge.
Serves 2.

Absolute Organix is our favourite pea protein and The Real Thing is our favourite green powder brand. This is a very thin, delicious, protein rich drink.

Silver Lining Breakfast Smoothie

Ingredients

3 T pea protein powder
1 t hemp seeds
1 T green powder (wheatgrass, barley grass, sea vegetables, chlorella, spirulina, etc.)
1 C almond milk or rice milk
1 C ice
½ C water
2 medjool dates, pitted

Method

Blend the ingredients in a high-speed blender until smooth.
Serve chilled.
Lasts up to 2 days in the fridge.
Serves 2.
Freezes well.

Salads

leafy greens, sprouts, avocado...
natures best healthy offerings
in a bowl

Sprouts... easy to grow high in minerals.

Asian Seaweed Salad

Radish and Avocado Salad

Asian Seaweed Salad

Salad Ingredients

½ C seaweed, soaked in water for 5 minutes,
cut into small strips (hijiki, wakame, kombu, arame)
½ cucumber, peeled and sliced
¼ C radish, very thinly sliced
¼ C pear, thinly sliced
1 medium orange, peeled and segmented
½ C rocket

Orange Dressing Ingredients

¼ C orange juice, fresh
1 t orange zest (grated orange skin)
2 T tahini (sesame seed paste)
2 T tamari (wheat-free soy sauce)
½ t sesame oil

Method

Combine salad ingredients in a bowl.
Blend dressing ingredients and toss into salad. Garnish with one teaspoon sesame seeds and fresh coriander.
Lasts a day in the fridge.
Serve 2.

Radish and Avocado Salad

Ingredients

2 C cucumber, peeled and diced
1 C radish, diced
2 avocados, peeled and diced
¼ C sunflower sprouts, cleaned
2 T olive oil
2 T lemon juice, fresh
1 T apple cider vinegar
1 t liquid sweetener of your choice
Salt to taste
Black pepper to taste

Method

Toss the ingredients in a bowl.
Sprinkle with black pepper and serve.
Lasts up to 2 days in the fridge.
Serves 4.

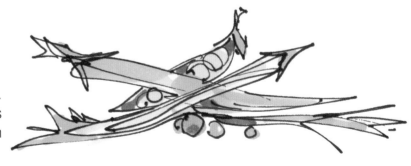

Leafy Greens Salad

Leafy Greens Salad

Salad Ingredients

3 C mixed leafy salad greens
1 C rocket, fresh
1 small carrot, peeled, julienned
¼ red pepper, finely chopped
¼ C cucumber, finely chopped
¼ C broccoli florets, finely chopped
1 ripe tomato, chopped
½ C fresh sprouts (mung, alfalfa, fenugreek,
pea, sunflower, buckwheat, etc.)
½ avocado, chopped

Dressing Ingredients

½ C cashews
1 C olive oil
¼ C lemon juice, fresh
1 garlic clove, peeled
1 T lemon zest
1 t liquid sweetener of your choice
Pinch of salt

Method

Toss the salad ingredients in a bowl.
Blend the dressing ingredients on high incorporating
the olive oil last. Taste the dressing for flavour.
Pour it over the salad and toss lightly.
This dressing lasts a week in the fridge.
Serves 4.

the art of making a good salad:
Do not over toss... keep it light
and fresh and use fresh salad.

Creamy Potato Salad

Creamy Potato Salad

Ingredients

6 medium potatoes, peeled and cooked until firm
1 C peas, fresh or frozen
1 C vegan cheese (see recipe on page 169)
3 T olive oil
Salt to taste
Black pepper to taste
Pinch chili flakes (optional)

Method

Cut the potatoes into medium chunks about 2 cm squared.
Toss all the ingredients in a bowl. Serve at room temperature.
Lasts up to 4 days in the fridge in a sealed container.
Serves 6.

Spinach Salad with Cranberries and Almonds

Spinach Salad with Cranberries and Almonds

Ingredients

1 bunch of spinach, stems removed and thinly sliced
½ C cranberries, dried *
2 T red onion, minced
½ C almond flakes, blanched
3 T sesame seeds
2 T poppy seeds
3 T apple cider vinegar
2 T xylitol (diabetic sweetener)
½ C olive oil
Paprika to taste
Salt to taste
Black pepper to taste

Method

Mix spinach, cranberries, almonds, onion and seeds in a bowl.
Whisk the remaining ingredients to make the salad dressing in a separate bowl.
Toss all the ingredients and serve immediately.
This salad does not keep well.
Serves 4.

* Make sure the cranberries have no sugar added.

Seaweed and Rocket Salad

Casalinga's Spinach Salad

Seaweed and Rocket Salad

Salad Ingredients

¼ C seaweed (wakame, hijiki or dulse), soaked for 5 minutes, roughly chopped
2 C rocket, fresh
1 C tomatoes, diced
½ C cucumber, diced
4 T sesame seeds

Dressing Ingredients

4 T olive oil
5 T tahini (sesame seed paste)
3 T lemon juice, fresh
1 t curry powder, medium
Salt to taste

Method

Blend the dressing ingredients, incorporating the olive oil last.
Pour the dressing over the salad ingredients, toss and serve.
Lasts a day in the fridge.
Serves 2.

Casalinga's Spinach Salad

A Family Favourite

Salad Ingredients

3 C spinach, finely sliced, stems removed
½ C croutons (bought or home-made)
1 avocado, chopped
¾ orange, peeled and segmented
2 T pine nuts, roasted

Dressing Ingredients

1 T liquid sweetener of your choice
2 T tamari (wheat-free soy sauce)
1 T curry powder, medium
3 T olive oil
1 T lemon juice

Method

Toss the salad ingredients in a bowl.
Blend the dressing ingredients in a blender until smooth.
Pour the dressing onto the salad.
Serve immediately.
This salad does not keep well.
Serves 3.

Seaweed is very high in iodine & iron and very good for the thyroid.

Vegan Coleslaw

Coleslaw

Ingredients

2 C red cabbage, finely sliced
2½ C green cabbage, finely sliced
2 apples, julienned (thinly sliced)
2 medium carrots, peeled, julienned
¼ C raisins, soaked for 5 minutes
½ white onion, finely sliced (optional)
½ C vegan cheese (see recipe on page 169)
Salt to taste
White pepper to taste

Method

Toss the ingredients in a bowl and serve immediately.
This salad does not keep well.
Serves 6.

the basis of a coleslaw...
a perfect home-grown cabbage!

Avocado, Mango and Tomato Salad

Ingredients

2 avocados, peeled
1 ½ mangoes, peeled
(Heidi mangoes are the best)
2 tomatoes, ripe, firm
1 T olive oil
¼ C rocket, fresh
Salt to taste
White pepper to taste

Method

Chop the ingredients into 2 cm square pieces. Mix in a bowl with the olive oil, salt and pepper.
Garnish with fresh rocket and serve.
Lasts up to 2 days in the fridge.
Serves 3.

Avocado, Mango and Tomato Salad

This is my absolute favourite salad. Three of my best fruits in a bowl.

Tuscan Kale Salad

Tuscan Kale Salad

Salad Ingredients

3 C kale leaves, fresh
1 medium carrot, peeled and julienned (thinly sliced)
½ red pepper, julienned

Dressing Ingredients

½ C cashews
½ red pepper, deseeded
½ C olive oil
¼ C maple syrup
¼ C lemon juice, fresh
½ C water
2 T apple cider vinegar
2 T tahini (sesame seed paste)
1 t ginger, peeled and diced
1 t chili, dried
Salt to taste

Method

Tear the kale leaves into medium sized pieces and remove all the stems.
Set it aside in a bowl with the carrot and red pepper. Blend the dressing ingredients until smooth. Massage the dressing into the kale by hand. This helps to break down the kale and makes it easier to digest.
Lasts up to 3 days in the fridge.
Serves 4.

Tomato Caprese

Ingredients

2 tomatoes, ripe, firm
¼ C basil leaves
¼ C vegan cheese
(see recipe on page 169)
2 T vegan parmesan
(see recipe on page 162)
1 T olive oil
Salt to taste
Black pepper to taste

Method

Slice the well-ripened tomatoes into
1 cm thick pieces and lay them on a
plate. Top with vegan cheese, fresh
basil leaves and sprinkle with vegan
parmesan, salt and pepper.
Serve at room temperature.
Lasts up to a day in the fridge.
Serves 2.

Waldorf Salad

Ingredients

2 C rocket, fresh
1 small apple, cut into small quarters,
core removed
¼ C raisins, soaked for 5 minutes
¼ C walnuts, roughly chopped
¼ C celery, finely chopped
¼ C vegan cheese
(see recipe on page 169)
1 T olive oil (optional)

Salt to taste

Method

Toss the ingredients in a bowl and
serve.
This salad does not last well.
Serves 4.

Panzanella Salad

½ C bread, large chunks
1 C tomato, roughly chopped
1 C cucumber, roughly chopped
¼ C red onion, roughly chopped
1 garlic clove, finely chopped
¼ C basil, chopped
3 T olive oil
1½ T red wine vinegar
Salt to taste
Black pepper to taste

Method

Toss the ingredients in a bowl.
Toast the bread lightly in a pan with a drop of olive oil.
Lasts up to 2 days in the fridge.
Serves 4.

Fig, Rocket and Walnut Salad

Ingredients

1 C black figs, ripe quartered
1½ C rocket, fresh
3 T walnuts, chopped
3 T olive oil
1 T vegan cheese
(see recipe on page 169)
1 t liquid sweetener of your choice
Salt to taste
Black pepper to taste

Method

Toss the ingredient in a bowl.
Serve fresh and slightly chilled.
This salad does not last well.
Serves 2.

Panzanella Salad

Lentil Salad

Ingredients

1¼ C brown lentils, sprouted or tinned
¼ C red cabbage, finely chopped
¼ C cherry tomatoes, halved
½ red onion, finely sliced
1 garlic clove, finely chopped
3 T parsley, stems removed and chopped
3 T chives, chopped
1 C rocket, fresh
3 T olive oil
1 T red wine vinegar
Salt to taste
Black pepper to taste

Method

Toss the ingredients in a bowl and serve.
Lasts up to 3 days in the fridge.
Serves 4.

Lentil Salad

Mozambique Butternut Salad

Ingredients

2 C raw butternut, grated or
spiralized into thin spaghetti
2 garlic cloves, chopped
¼ t fresh chili, deseeded, chopped
4 T olive oil
4 T fresh coriander or basil,
chopped
3 T lime or lemon juice
1 t liquid sweetener of your choice
1 T lime zest (grated lime skin)
3 T cashews, chopped

Method

Mix the ingredients in a bowl and
serve fresh with a slice of lime or
lemon.
Last 2 days in the fridge.
Serves 2.

Mozambique Butternut Salad

Brown Rice Salad

Brown Rice Salad

Salad Ingredients

3 C brown rice, cooked
½ C chickpeas, tinned or cooked
6 dates, pitted, chopped
¼ red pepper, chopped
¼ C celery, chopped
2 T pecans, chopped
¼ C sun-dried tomatoes, soaked for 10 minutes and chopped
3 T parsley, chopped

Dressing Ingredients

¾ C olive oil
3 T lemon juice, fresh
1 T red wine vinegar
2 T tamari (wheat-free say sauce)
1 t mustard (Hot English)
Salt to taste
Black pepper to taste

Method

Combine the dressing ingredients in a blender. Mix the salad ingredients in a bowl and toss with the dressing. Lasts up to 3 days in the fridge. Serves 4.

Caesar Salad

Salad Ingredients

1 cos lettuce, roughly chopped
3 T capers, chopped
2 radish, thinly sliced (optional)
¼ C croutons (bought or
home-made)

* Cos lettuce is also
known as Romaine

Dressing Ingredients

½ C cashews
¼ C macadamias
1 C water
4 T olive oil
3 dates, pitted
1 T tamari (wheat-free soy sauce)
2 T lemon juice, fresh
1 garlic clove, peeled
Salt to taste
Black pepper to taste

Method

Blend the dressing ingredients on
high until smooth.
Mix the capers into the dressing
after blending. This gives a
pleasant texture to the dressing.
In a bowl, place the chopped cos
lettuce and coat with the dressing.
Top with the croutons, finely sliced
radish and a crack of black pepper.
Lasts a day in the fridge.
Serves 3.

Mung Bean, Seaweed and Garlic Salad

Ingredients

1 C mung beans, sprouted
¼ C rocket, fresh
1 t tahini (sesame seed paste)
1 t garlic, chopped
2 T olive oil
2 T lemon juice
¼ C seaweed (kelp, wakame, hijiki)
soaked for 5 minutes, cut into small
pieces
Salt to taste
White pepper to taste

Method

Toss the ingredients in a bowl and
serve.
Lasts up to 3 days in the fridge.
Serves 2.

Broccoli and Sesame Salad

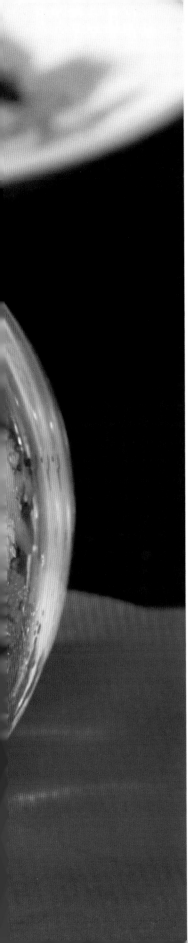

Broccoli and Sesame Salad

Ingredients

1 head broccoli
1 medium avocado, diced
2 T olive oil
1 T lemon juice, fresh
1 t English Mustard (or mustard of your choice)
1 T sesame seeds
1 T red onion, finely diced
1 T sunflower seeds, lightly roasted
1 t capers, chopped
1 T red pepper, finely chopped
Salt to taste
White pepper to taste

Method

Steam the whole broccoli head in a pot with 2 cm of
water in the bottom and a pinch of salt in the water.
Once the broccoli has cooled, cut the florets into medium
sized pieces and place in a bowl.
Add the rest of the ingredients and toss well.
Serve warm.
Lasts up to 2 days in the fridge.
Serves 4.

Raw Foods

enzyme rich, living uncooked foods... in their natural state

Raw Pizza

Base Ingredients

2 C buckwheat, hulled, soaked for 12 hours   *Rinse the buckwheat well.*
1½ C flaxseeds, ground
1½ C zucchini, chopped
1/2 C tomato, chopped
1/2 red onion, chopped
2 T tamari (wheat-free soy sauce)
¼ C olive oil   *The raw base lasts a week in the*
1 garlic clove, peeled   *fridge in a sealed container.*

Method

Process the base ingredients in a food processor until smooth.
Spread a thin layer (½ cm thick) on a dehydrator tray and dry
at 50 °C overnight or until dry.

Raw Tomato Sauce Ingredients *Freezes well.*

1 C tomatoes, chopped
1 C sundried tomatoes, soaked for 15 minutes
½ C liquid from soaked sundried tomatoes or tomato juice
¼ t mixed herbs, dried
Salt to taste
Black pepper to taste

Method

Blend the tomato sauce ingredients until smooth. Add the
herbs at the end for a better texture.

Marinate the vegetables of your choice for the pizza toppings.
Mushrooms, onions, broccoli, peppers, carrots, etc work well.
Marinate one cup of the vegetable mix in ⅓ cup tamari and ½
cup olive oil overnight.

Raw Pizza

To Assemble the Pizza

Top the base with a thin layer of raw tomato sauce.
Place some of the marinated vegetables on top.
Add sliced avocado and a few olives.
Top with vegan cheese (see recipe on page 169).
Garnish with rocket, black pepper and a drizzle of olive oil.
This pizza does not last well. Assemble to eat.

Rice Paper Rolls

Rice Paper Rolls

*Made with rice paper available
from most Asian shops and
Leafy Greens' Store.
* This is not raw!*

Raw Rice Ingredients

1 medium cauliflower, chopped
¼ C macadamia nuts
1 T olive oil
2 T lemon juice
1 t liquid sweetener of your choice
Salt to taste

Method

Pulse the ingredients in a food
processor until a rice-like consistency
is achieved. Squeeze the mixture in a
nut milk bag to remove all excess liquid.

Dip the sheet of rice paper in boiling
water for 2 seconds and place on a
board. Take ½ a cup of the raw rice
and lay it on top of the rice paper in
the center. Top with sliced vegetables
of your choice (peppers, avocado,
zucchini, cucumber, celery, carrots,
mint, sprouts, etc).
Roll the rice paper over the filling and
slice the roll in half.

** Normal white sushi rice or rice
noodles can be used in place of the
raw rice in this recipe.*

Sweet Chili Dipping Sauce Ingredients

1 C tamari (wheat-free soy sauce)
1 T liquid sweetener of your choice
1 t chili powder
1 t fresh red chili, chopped (remove
seeds for a milder sauce)

Method

Mix the dipping sauce ingredients
in a bowl.

Homemade Ginger Ingredients

¼ C ginger, peeled and thinly sliced
on a mandolin
½ C apple cider vinegar
1 t beetroot juice, fresh

Method

Add the ginger ingredients to a glass
jar and store in the fridge for up to 2
months.

Plating: serve three rice paper rolls
with a small bowl of the dipping
sauce and a few pieces of ginger on
the side. You can also serve some
shop-bought wasabi with the dish.
The rice paper rolls do not last well in
the fridge.
Serves 4.

Pistachio Pesto filled Brown Mushrooms

Pesto Ingredients

2 C pistachios,
soaked for 10 minutes in water
¾ C olive oil
1 C basil leaves
2 spinach leaves, stems removed
5 garlic cloves
Salt to taste

Other Ingredients

4 large brown mushrooms
¼ C sun dried tomatoes,
soaked for 5 minutes

Method

Combine the pesto ingredients in a food processor until chunky but well incorporated. Add 3 tablespoons of pesto to the top of each brown mushroom, sprinkle with finely chopped sun dried tomatoes. Serve at room temperature with a simple green salad. The pesto lasts up to a week in the fridge. Serves 4.

Pistachios can be substituted with pecans, walnuts, macadamias or pumpkin seeds.

Pistachio Pesto filled Brown Mushrooms

Raw Wraps

Ingredients

1 C fresh juice of your choice*
2 C coconut meat
Salt to taste

Method

Blend the wrap ingredients until extremely smooth.
Spread the mixture very thinly (about 2 mm thick) onto a solid sheet and dehydrate for 8 hours at 45°C.

Fill with green salad and creamy thyme dressing (see recipe on page 140), sprinkle with hemp seeds and serve immediately.
The dry wraps last up to a week in the fridge individually wrapped in wax paper. The wrap does not last once it is filled with salad.
Makes 2 wraps.

The best versions of this recipe make use of sweet ripe tomatoes, mangoes, spinach or butternut juice.

Raw Wraps

Green Soup

Green Soup

Ingredients

1½ C green juice (kale, spinach, parsley, cabbage, lettuce, lemon)
1 medium avocado, peeled
1 T olive oil
1 garlic clove, peeled
2 basil leaves, fresh
½ t turmeric powder
Salt to taste

Method

Blend on high until smooth.
Enjoy chilled in a bowl.
Lasts a day in the fridge.
Serve with a few mung bean sprouts or fresh chopped herbs.
Freezes well.
Serves 2.

* This soup is great when you have green juice in the fridge and you are in the mood for a light, quick and easy dinner.

Tomato Gazpacho

Tomato Gazpacho

Ingredients

8 tomatoes, blanched, peeled
1 red pepper, chopped
¼ C celery, chopped
½ onion, peeled, chopped
4 garlic cloves, peeled
¼ C olive oil
4 sundried tomatoes, soaked for 15 minutes.
Salt to taste
Black pepper to taste

Method

Blanch the tomatoes in a pot of boiling water for 2 minutes.
Remove from the heat, allow to cool and peel. Process the ingredients in a food processor until fairly smooth.
Serve chilled with fresh bread.
Lasts up to 3 days in the fridge.
Freezes well.
Serves 6.

Chickpea and Sweet Potato
Falafels with Citrus Cream

Chickpea and Sweet Potato Falafels with Citrus Cream

Falafel Ingredients

¾ C chickpeas, sprouted* or tinned
¾ C sunflower seeds, finely ground
¾ C almonds, finely ground
¼ C sweet potato, diced, raw
¼ onion, peeled & diced
¼ C olive oil
2 T lemon juice, fresh
⅓ C tamari (wheat-free soy sauce)
3 garlic cloves, peeled
2 T curry powder, meduim

Use sprouted chickpeas for a 100 % raw dish.

Method

Process the ingredients in a food processor until smooth.
Scoop out into even scoops (2 tablespoons) and dehydrate at 45°C for 6 hours or until crispy on the outside and still soft on the inside.
Makes approximately 24 falafels.
Freezes well.

Citrus Cream Ingredients

1 C olive oil
2 T cashews
¼ C lemon juice
¼ C orange juice
2 garlic cloves, chopped
1 T orange zest (grated orange skin)
Salt to taste

Method

Combine Citrus Cream ingredients together in a blender.
Adding the olive oil last slowly in order to achieve a creamy consistency. Serve with the falafels and a fresh green salad.
Falafels last up to 4 days covered in the fridge.
Cream lasts up to a week in the fridge.
Makes approximately 1 cup of cream.
Freezes well.

Mom's Spicy Avocado Soup

Ingredients

2 avocados, ripe, peeled
2 garlic cloves, peeled
4 T onion, peeled, chopped
½ C water
2 T olive oil
1 t turmeric powder
Chili flakes to taste
Salt to taste

Method

Blend the ingredients until smooth.
Garnish with dulse, fresh sprouts and
pink peppercorns.
Lasts a day in the fridge.
Serves 2.

Zucchini Carpaccio

Ingredients

2 large zucchini, thinly sliced
¼ C olive oil
3 T lemon juice
1 small celery stalk, thinly sliced
2 small spring onions, chopped
Salt to taste
Black pepper to taste
1 t vegan parmesan (see recipe on page 162).

A mandolin is the best piece of equipment to use to slice the vegetables in this recipe.

Method

Place the thinly sliced zucchini on a baking tray and marinate with the olive oil, lemon juice, salt and pepper. Let it stand for 10 minutes. Plating: lay the zucchini neatly on a plate and sprinkle with the celery and spring onions and vegan parmesan. Serve immediately.
This does not last in the fridge.
Serves 2.

Cabbage Kim Chi

Ingredients

1 head Chinese cabbage
1/4 C salt
3 C water
6 garlic cloves, grated
1 t fresh ginger, grated
1 t liquid sweetener of your choice
3 T chili flakes
8 small radish, sliced
4 spring onions

** Fermented foods are
high in probiotics
that balance
the stomach flora.*

Method

Cut the cabbage into 5 cm pieces. Place the cabbage and salt in a large bowl. Massage the salt into the cabbage until it starts to soften. Add enough water to cover the cabbage. Put a plate on top of the cabbage and weigh it down with something heavy. Let it stand for 1-2 hours. Rinse the cabbage with water until the salt is removed and drain it in a colander until fairly dry. Squeeze any remaining water from the cabbage and return it to a bowl.   In a separate bowl, combine the garlic, ginger, chili and sweetener to form a paste.

Using your hands, mix the paste along with the radish and spring onions, into the vegetables until they are well combined.

Pack the kim chi into a one liter glass jar, pressing it down until the brine (liquid) rises to cover the vegetables. Leave at least 5 cm of space at the top of the jar. Seal the jar with the lid.

Let the jar stand at room temperature for 2 - 4 days (depending on temperature). Check the kim chi, pressing down on the vegetables with a clean spoon to keep them under the brine. This also releases gases produced during fermentation. When the kim chi is ready (after about 4 days), place the jar in the fridge.

The kim chi is then ready to eat. It lasts up to 3 weeks in the fridge.

Artichoke Paté

Ingredients

5 fresh artichokes
¼ C olive oil
1 garlic clove, peeled
2 T fresh thyme, chopped
1 T fresh parsley, chopped
1 T nutritional yeast (a deactivated yeast that is very high in vitamin B12 and protein)
Salt to taste
Black pepper to taste

Method

Clean the artichokes by rinsing them and removing the outer dry leaves and cutting off the spiky edges.
Steam the artichokes until soft.
Process the ingredients in a food processor until chunky.
Lasts up to 4 days in the fridge.

My father has had his artichoke plants since 1984.

Marinated Vegetable Skewers

Marinated Vegetable Skewers

Skewer Ingredients

3 medium zucchini
6 mushrooms, cleaned
1 tomato
1 carrot, peeled
1 red pepper
1 yellow pepper
½ a small butternut, peeled

Method

Chop the ingredients into 2 - 3 cm squares
and place on skewer sticks.

Marinade Ingredients

1 C olive oil
¼ C tamari (wheat-free soy sauce)
2 T chili powder, dried
1 T mixed herbs, dried
1 garlic clove, peeled
1 t liquid sweetener of your choice
Salt to taste
Black pepper to taste

Method

Mix the ingredients and place in a large bowl with your skewers.
Allow them to marinate overnight. Dehydrate the skewers at 45°C
the next day for 8 hours or until soft.
Serve with a side salad.
Lasts up to 3 days in the fridge.
Serves 2.

Cooked Vegan

Some of our favourite croquettes
& curry, something warm and
comforting every now and again...

Eggplant and Pesto Pizza

Use any bought or homemade pizza base, gluten-free or regular, add the following toppings:

Ingredients

3 T basil pesto * (bought or made)
Half a medium eggplant, sliced fairly thin (½ cm pieces)
4 T caramelized onions (see recipe on page 155)
¼ C mushrooms, chopped (brown or button)
3 T red pepper, chopped
4 T vegan cheese (see recipe on page 169)
8 fresh basil leaves, stems removed
Salt to taste
Black pepper to taste

Optional Extras for Spice

Pinch of ground cloves
Pinch of ground nutmeg

Method

Pre-cook the pizza base for 2 - 3 minutes in a hot oven (250°C or more). Remove from oven and spread pesto thinly on the base right up to the edges (as you would do with a tomato paste).
Add the eggplant, mushrooms, onions and peppers to the pizza.

Spread the vegan cheese on top and bake the pizza for a further 2 - 4 minutes in the hot oven until golden. Remove from the oven, garnish with basil leaves. Slice the pizza and serve hot with chili on the side.

* Basil Pesto Recipe

2 C basil leaves
½ C cashews or pine nuts
3 T olive oil
2 T lemon juice, fresh
1 garlic clove, peeled

Salt to taste
White pepper to taste

Method

Blend the ingredients until slightly chunky.

Spinach Croquettes

Spinach Croquettes

Filling Ingredients

1½ large bunches of spinach,
stems removed
¼ t bicarbonate of soda
2 liters of water
1 C zucchini grated
2 large carrots, grated
¼ red pepper, finely chopped

½ onion, finely chopped
2 garlic cloves, finely chopped
2 T olive oil
Salt to taste
Black pepper to taste
Pinch chili powder (optional)
¾ C Napoli sauce
(see recipe on page 167)
1 T dried oregano
2 T breadcrumbs

Boil the spinach with the bicarbonate of soda in 2 liters of water. Remove the spinach from the pot and place in ice-cold water to retain the green colour.

When the cooked spinach is cold, remove from the water and drain well (discard the water). Set the spinach aside. To a separate pan, add the carrots, peppers, onion, garlic, olive oil, salt and pepper and pan fry until soft and golden. Add the spinach and zucchini to the pan and cook until soft.

Remove from heat and add the Napoli sauce, oregano and breadcrumbs. Mix until well combined.

Divide mixture into small batches and roll into oval shapes.

To Assemble the Croquettes

On one tray, place 1 cup dry buckwheat flour. On a second tray place 1 cup breadcrumbs.

Take the spinach mixture in one hand and dip it in the buckwheat binder, then in the dry buckwheat flour, then back in buckwheat binder and roll in the breadcrumbs.

Once all the croquettes have been rolled, you can pan fry, bake or deep-fry it. Serve hot!

Lasts up to 5 days in the fridge.

Freezes well.

Makes 12 to 16 croquettes.

Buckwheat Binder Ingredients

½ C Buckwheat flour
1¼ C water

Binder Method

Whisk the buckwheat binder ingredients until smooth.

Nick's Quinoa Bowl

Ingredients

1 C quinoa
3 C water
2 T tamari (wheat-free soy sauce)
1 T lemon juice, fresh
1 t sesame oil
Pinch cayenne pepper
¼ C red cabbage, finely chopped
¼ C broccoli, finely chopped
¼ C onions, finely chopped
¼ C peas, fresh or frozen
¼ C mushrooms, chopped
2 T carrots, peeled and grated
2 garlic cloves, chopped
2 T olive oil
Salt to taste
Black pepper to taste

Method

Cook the quinoa in two cups of boiling water with a pinch of salt. Drain the quinoa and add the tamari, lemon juice, sesame oil and pepper to taste. Mix well. In a seperate pan sauté all the vegetables. Once the vegetables are cooked through, add the cooked quinoa and toss well. Garnish with a sprinkle of black sesame seeds, bean sprouts, toasted cashews or a quarter of a diced avocado.
Lasts up to 3 days in the fridge in a sealed container.
Serves 4.

Nick's Quinoa Bowl

Brown Rice Moussaka

Base Ingredients

2 C brown rice
¼ C green peas (fresh or frozen)
¼ C carrots, peeled, finely cubed
¼ yellow or red pepper, finely chopped
½ small onion, peeled, diced
3 T olive oil
2 garlic cloves, finely chopped
1 T parsley, stems removed, chopped
Salt to taste
White pepper to taste

Base Method

Bring 4 cups of water to the boil, add a pinch of salt and the rice. Keep the lid of the pot closed until the rice is cooked. This may take up to 40 minutes to cook thoroughly. Pan fry the rest of the ingredients until fairly soft. Once soft toss with the cooked brown rice until well combined. Push the mixture into a baking tray about 5 cm deep.

Topping Ingredients

1 C coconut cream
1 T potato or buckwheat flour
1 T mixed herbs, dried
Salt to taste

Topping Method

Blend topping ingredients on high. Spread the topping about 1cm thick on the rice and bake in an oven until golden brown. This takes approximately 10 - 15 minutes at 180°C. Season with a sprinkle of paprika and olive oil. Lasts up to 4 days in the fridge. Freezes well.
Serves 5.

Brown Rice Moussaka

Vegan Burger Patty

Vegan Burger Patty

Patty Ingredients

¼ C onions, finely diced
¼ C carrots, finely chopped
¼ C red peppers, finely chopped
¼ C mushrooms, finely chopped
2 garlic cloves, minced
3 C quinoa, cooked, organic
2 t cumin, ground
2 t chili powder
2 T coconut oil or olive oil
Salt to taste
¾ C beans (brown, black, chickpeas)
¼ C bread crumbs

Method

Cook quinoa: two cups of water to one cup of quinoa with a pinch of salt. It cooks fast (10 to 15 minutes). Keep an eye on it and add more water if needed. Put the quinoa aside.

Heat coconut or olive oil in a pan and sauté the onions, garlic, mushrooms, peppers and carrots until soft. Add the cumin, chili, salt and stir. Remove pan from the heat and let it cool.

Once all the ingredients have cooled, add it to the food processor with the quinoa, beans and breadcrumbs and pulse.

Butternut Soup

* Pumpkin can also be used instead of the butternut in this recipe.

Keep the mixture fairly textured.

Form the mixture into 7cm x 2cm patties.

Pan-fry or bake the patties.

Serve on a roll with onion, tomato, avocado, lettuce and vegan cheese (see recipe on page 169).

These patties freeze well.
Makes 6 to 8 patties.

Butternut Soup

Ingredients

1 butternut, peeled and cubed
1 C coconut milk
1 ½ T fresh herbs
(sage, rosemary, oregano)
2 garlic cloves, peeled (optional)
Salt to taste
Black pepper to taste

Method

Blend the ingredients on high. Heat in a pot. Serve hot with bread or crackers and vegan butter (see recipe on page 163). Lasts up to 3 days in the fridge. Freezes well. Serves 3.

Zucchini Fries

Zucchini Fries

Ingredients

12 medium zucchini
2 T salt
1 C flour (spelt or gluten free)
¼ C coconut or olive oil
White pepper to taste

Method

Slice the zucchini into the size of French fries and cover them with the salt. Let it stand for an hour to drain off the excesswater. Rinse off the excess salt. Dip the fries in the flour and pan-fry until golden for 5 to 7 minutes.

Serve hot, with a sprinkle of coarse salt and white pepper on top.

Zucchini Fritters

Zucchini Fritters

Ingredients

2 C zucchini, grated
2 T salt
½ C white onion, peeled, finely chopped
½ C parsley, stems removed, finely chopped
½ C spelt flour, stone-ground
2 T buckwheat flour mixed with 3 T water (acts as an egg replacement)
¼ C coconut oil for frying

Method

Place zucchini in a dish, cover with the salt and let it stand for 30 minutes.
Rinse off all the excess salt and water.
Mix all the ingredients in a bowl and form 5 cm round patties.
Pan fry the fritters for about 4 minutes on each side or until golden.
Serve with chopped fresh chives and vegan cheese (see recipe on page 151). Lasts up to 1 day in the fridge. Makes 12 fritters.

Cabbage Wraps

Cabbage Wraps

Wrap Ingredients

6 cabbage leaves, whole
4 C water
½ t bicarbonate of soda.

* Replace cabbage with kale or spinach leaves for variation.

Method

Boil the large whole cabbage leaves in 4 cups of water with ½ teaspoon bicarbonate of soda in the water. This helps to keep the green colour of the cabbage leaves.

Filling Ingredients

½ C Napoli Sauce (see recipe on page 167)
2 carrots, peeled, julienned
¼ red pepper, finely chopped
¼ yellow pepper, finely chopped
½ onion, peeled, finely diced
2 garlic cloves, finely chopped
2 T olive oil
1 C cabbage (inner soft leaves), finely chopped
2 tomatoes, chopped
4 T breadcrumbs (bought or home-made)
Salt to taste
White pepper to taste

Method

Pan-fry the filling ingredients until soft. Place one of the whole cooked cabbage leaves on a flat board. Cut out the main large vein and join the edges so that you have one flat leaf with no gaps. Place half a cup of the filling onto one side of the leaf and roll the cabbage leaf over, cutting off all uneven edges. Place the rolls in a medium sized baking dish and top with half a cup of Italian Napoli Sauce (see recipe on page 169) and sprinkle with 4 tablespoons of breadcrumbs. Bake in the oven for 15 minutes at 180°C or until golden brown.
Serve hot with green salad or rice and top with some of the sauce from your baking tray.
Lasts up to 2 days in the fridge.
Serves 3.

Vegan Cauliflower Cheese

Ingredients

1 head of cauliflower
½ C vegan cheese (see recipe on page 169)
3 T vegan butter (see recipe on page 163)
2 C coconut milk
2 T buckwheat flour
1 T nutmeg, ground
1 T paprika, ground
Salt to taste
White pepper to taste

Method

Steam the cauliflower in a pot with just a centimeter or so of water. Cook through, but leave it a little crunchy.
Allow it to cool and then break up the florets into medium sized pieces.
In a separate pot, make the white sauce by mixing the vegan butter, coconut milk, nutmeg and buckwheat flour, bring it to a light boil.
Toss the steamed cauliflower in the white sauce and place it a baking dish, top with the vegan cheese and paprika and bake it in the oven at 200°C for 10 minutes or until golden brown on the top.
Lasts up to a week in the fridge.
Serves 4.

* This dish when blended with water and coconut milk to thin it out, makes a lovely soup!

Butternut Gratin

Ingredients

2 large butternuts, peeled and cut into thin rounds (about ½ cm thick)
15 fresh sage leaves, chopped
6 garlic cloves, chopped
1 C coconut milk
1 t curry powder, mild
½ t turmeric powder
4 T vegan parmesan (see recipe on page 162)
Salt to taste
Black pepper to taste

Method

Layer the butternut, herbs and garlic in a baking dish, top with coconut milk. Bake in the oven at 180°C for 20 - 25 minutes until golden on top but firm.
Serve hot with green salad on the side and sprinkle with lots of vegan parmesan.
Last up to 3 days in the fridge.
Serves 6.

* Substitute the butternut with pumpkin or sweet potato for variation.

Butternut Gratin

Minestrone Soup

This is always a family favourite.

Ingredients

2 carrots, peeled, cubed
2 celery stalks, roughly chopped
½ onion, roughly chopped
1 medium potato, peeled, cubed
Black pepper to taste
3 T vegetable stock powder
2 C boiling water
1 C broccoli florets, chopped
2 tomatoes, diced
1 C zucchini, diced
1 t mixed herbs, dried
Salt to taste
¾ C red kidney beans
½ C baby spinach, chopped

Method

Pan-fry the carrots, celery, onion and potato in a pot until fairly soft and lightly golden. Season with salt and pepper.

Add the vegetable stock, water and the broccoli, tomatoes, zucchini and mixed herbs. Cook slowly in the pot, adding water slowly as needed to achieve a soup-like consistency.

This normally takes about 1 hour in a medium sized pot on a low heat. 5 minutes before removing the soup from the heat, add the beans and spinach. Add 1 teaspoon of basil pesto at the end for a rich and creamy taste, as well as 2 tablespoons of Napoli sauce (see recipe on page 167). Serve this soup hot with fresh bread or crackers.

Lasts up to 5 days in the fridge.
Freezes well.
Serves 12.

Minestrone Soup

Chickpea Curry

Ingredients

4 large carrots, peeled and chopped
3 red peppers, chopped
4 zucchini, chopped
3 tomatoes, chopped
2 potatoes, peeled and chopped
3 garlic cloves, peeled and chopped
2 onions, peeled and chopped
1 T olive oil

Method

Sauté the ingredients in a pot until the potatoes are nearly cooked through.

* Add the softer vegetables later as they cook faster.

Then Add

2 T curry powder, medium
1 t turmeric powder
2 C coconut milk
3 C chickpeas, tinned
1 C green peas, fresh or frozen
Salt to taste
White pepper to taste

Method

Heat everything thoroughly and serve with brown rice or quinoa and Indian condiments such as chutney, tomato relish, coconut flakes or sliced banana.
Garnish with parsley or coriander.
Lasts up to 4 days in the fridge.
Serves 6.

Chickpea Curry

Leek & Jerusalem Artichoke Soup

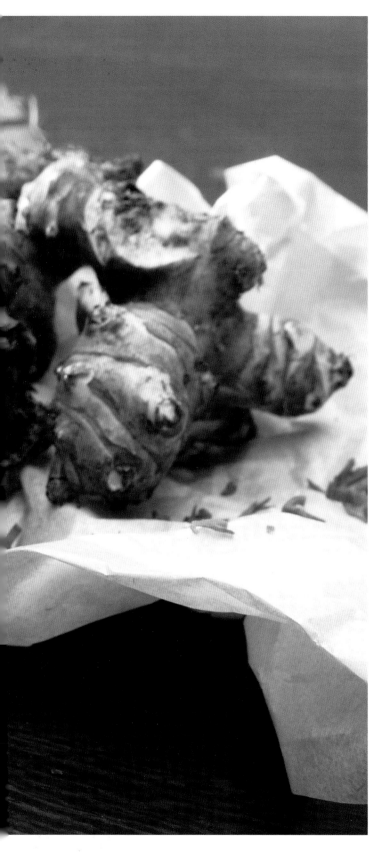

Leek and Jerusalem Artichoke Soup

Ingredients

4 C Jerusalem Artichokes, cleaned
 but not peeled
1 leek, cleaned
1½ C water
1 t liquid sweetener of your choice
2 C coconut milk
Salt to taste
White pepper to taste

Method

Boil the leeks and Jerusalem
Artichokes in the water.
Cool slightly, then blend until smooth.
Mix in the coconut milk and sweetener and
season with salt and pepper.
Heat to serve.
Lasts up to 5 days in the fridge.
Freezes well.
Serves 5.

* Jerusalem Artichokes also known
as sunroot or sunchoke is a
species of sunflower. It looks like
ginger but has a potato-like
flavour. It is an excellent source
of dietary fibre and fairly easy to
cultivate.

Onion Tart

Pastry Ingredients

1½ C cake flour, stone-ground
½ C water
½ t baking powder
1 T vegan butter (see recipe on page 163)
2 T olive oil
Salt to taste

Filling Ingredients

10 onions, chopped
1 ¼ C water
1 T buckwheat flour
½ C olive oil
1 T caraway seeds
Salt to taste
Black pepper to taste

Pastry Method

Mix pastry ingredients until soft. Form one dough ball. If the dough is sticky, add a little flour to make it softer. Roll out the dough 1 cm thick. Line a 30 cm x 25 cm baking dish with olive oil and place the dough mixture in the baking dish, raising the edges of the dough up the dish. Blind bake the pastry until lightly cooked for 5 minutes at 200°C.
Remove from oven and let it cool for 5 minutes.

Filling Method

Pan-fry the onions in olive oil and 1 cup of water until the onions are very soft (15 minutes). Add the caraway seeds, salt and pepper and cook for another minute. Add the buckwheat flour mixed in a quarter cup of water and add it to the onion mixture and let it bind. Remove from heat and allow to stand for a further 5 minutes to bind well.
Place the onion mixture into the pastry base and bake in the oven at 200°C for 20 minutes or until golden on top.
Lasts up to to 3 days in the fridge.
Serves 8.

Onion Tart

131

Bruno's Potato Rösti

Bruno's Potato Rösti

Ingredients

4 medium potatoes
4 T coconut oil
Salt to taste
Pinch black pepper
½ lemon
1 T fresh herbs, chopped (sage, parsley, rosemary, etc)
1 T vegan cheese (see recipe on page 169)

Method

Parboil the potatoes for 9 minutes until flaky but still a bit firm. Let the potatoes cool. (This step can be done the day before to save time). Grate the potato on a large grater, and add salt and black pepper.

Cover the base of a non-stick pan with the melted coconut oil and add the potatoes. Toss the grated potato until it is well coated with coconut oil. Use chopsticks to toss in order to keep the potatoes light and airy.

Gently shape and even the mixture out in the pan but do not push the mixture down. Cook on medium heat until a golden brown crust is formed. This should take about 6 minutes. Flip the rösti and pan-fry for a further 5 minutes.

Serve with fresh chopped herbs, a cheek of lemon and a dash of vegan cheese (see recipe on page 169).
Lasts a day in the fridge.
Serves 6.

* Hint: Circle the rösti around in the pan until you hear a scratching sound, then it is ready to flip.

Potato Curry

Ingredients

3 potatoes, peeled and cubed
3 sweet potatoes, peeled and cubed
6 tomatoes, fresh, chopped
2 C spinach, stems removed, chopped
½ onion, peeled and chopped
1 C coconut milk
2 T curry powder, medium
2 garlic cloves, finely chopped
4 T coconut oil
Salt to taste

Method

Pan fry the onion and garlic in the oil. Add the curry powder, tomatoes and salt. Stir the ingredients until it forms a thick sauce.

In a seperate pot, boil the potatoes, sweet potatoes and the spinach until cooked through. Drain and set aside.

Mix the ingredients in one pot, add the coconut milk and bring to a boil. Serve with brown rice and salad.

Lasts up to 4 days in the fridge. Freezes well. Serves 4.

Potato Curry

Carrot Soup

Ingredients

6 carrots, peeled
1 onion, chopped
2 leeks, chopped (white part only)
¼ C olive oil
2 C vegetable stock
Pinch salt
Pinch white pepper
Pinch turmeric
Pinch coriander seeds, ground
¼ C coriander, fresh, chopped (add only at the end)

Method

Pan-fry the carrots, onion and leeks in the olive oil until soft. Add the vegetable stock and the spices. Boil until soft. Let the soup cool slightly and then blend it in a high-speed blender until completely smooth.
Serve with a drizzle of Salsa Verde (see recipe on page 159).
Lasts up to 4 days in the fridge.
Freezes well.
Serves 3.

Stinging Nettle Soup

Ingredients

2 C stinging nettles
1 C vegetable stock
½ onion, peeled
1 medium potato
½ C brown rice, cooked
2 T olive oil
1 garlic clove, peeled
Salt to taste
White pepper to taste

* Wear gloves when working with nettles.

Method

Boil the stinging nettles, rice, potato and onion in the vegetable stock until soft. Add the remaining ingredients and cook thoroughly. Blend the mixture on high until smooth and serve with a dash of vegan cheese on top (see recipe on page 169). Lasts up to 4 days in the fridge. Freezes well.
Serves 2.

Lou's African Chickpea Stew

Lou's African Chickpea Stew

Ingredients

1 ½ C chickpeas, tinned, drained
3 C chopped tomato, cooked
1 C vegetable stock
2 T olive oil
1 medium onion, diced
1 medium carrot, diced
1 small zucchini, diced
2 garlic cloves, crushed
9 dried apricots, chopped
¼ C raisins
2 t lemon zest, grated
1 t cumin, ground
¼ t cayenne pepper
4 T coriander, fresh, chopped
Salt to taste
Black pepper to taste

Method

Pan-fry the onion in the olive oil until soft and golden. Add the cumin, cayenne pepper, garlic, salt and pepper and cook for 5 minutes. Add the carrot, zucchini and tomato and cook for a further 5 minutes. Add the remaining ingredients. Cook until soft but not overdone. This should take another 10 minutes.
Serve hot with couscous or quinoa.
Garnish with the fresh coriander.
Lasts up to 3 days in the fridge.
Freezes well.
Serves 4.

Spelt Gnocchi

Ingredients

4 large potatoes, peeled, chopped
3 C spelt flour, stone-ground
Salt to taste

Method

Cook the potatoes until soft. Mash it and add the spelt flour. This process can be done in a food processor. Add the salt.
Roll out the dough onto a board that is well floured. Roll the dough out to 2 cm wide and 10 cm. Cut the gnocchi into 2 cm by 2 cm square pieces.
To cook, boil a pot of waterl and dunk the gnocchi in the pot. Cook for 3 minutes.
Remove with a sieve.
Toss the cooked gnocchi in a pan with a bit of Napoli sauce (see recipe on page 167) and serve with vegan parmesan (see recipe on page 162).
Lasts up to 3 days in fridge.
Serve 3.

* Spelt is an ancient grain. It has not been genetically modified, therefore it does not have the same severe side effects as wheat.

Fig and Walnut Loaf

Ingredients

500 g whole-wheat flour
10 g salt
5 g dry yeast
335 ml water
¾ C walnuts, roughly chopped
1 C dried figs, good quality

Method

Mix the ingredients in a bowl (except the walnuts and figs).
Knead the dough on a floured board. Stretch the dough out with each knead in order to activate the gluten. Roll and stretch the dough about 4 times. When the dough is ready, leave it stretched out and add the dried figs and walnuts. Roll the dough up like a Swiss roll. Set the dough aside and let it rise for one hour. Knock the dough back three times in the first hour. Then let the dough rise for another hour after being shaped into a bread loaf. Score the top of the loaf and bake it in a 220°C oven for 20 minutes.
It is best baked on a piece of stone or tile dusted with flour, with a bowl of ice in the oven to create steam and moisture. Turn the oven down to 200°C, place a spoon in oven door to keep it slightly ajar and bake for another 5 minutes. Serve with vegan butter (see recipe on page143.) Lasts up to 2 days. Freezes well. Makes 1 medium loaf.

Grilled Radicchio

Ingredients

2 medium heads of radicchio
¼ C olive oil
¼ C lemon juice, fresh
2 garlic cloves, crushed
Salt to taste

Method

Quarter the rasicchio.
Rub the radicchio with olive oil, lemon juice and garlic.
Grill it until golden brown on all sides.
Add salt and serve hot with green salad.
Lasts a day in the fridge.
Serves 2.

** Radicchio is a winter crop. The seeds are planted
in the summer and when winter comes around,
the head of the radicchio will form.
This is when it is ready to eat.*

Roasted Red Peppers

Ingredients

4 red peppers
½ C olive oil
1 T oregano, fresh, chopped
1 T sage, fresh, chopped
¼ C lemon juice, fresh
1 T parsley, fresh, chopped
Salt to taste
White pepper to taste

Method

Roast the red peppers in the oven until fairly soft, this normally takes about 15 minutes at 180°C. Remove the peppers and let them cool slightly in a bowl covered with foil (so that they sweat). Then peel off the skins. Cut the peppers into quarters and remove the seeds. Lay it in a baking dish and top with all the other ingredients. Serve with leafy greens and avocado.
Lasts up to 5 days in the fridge.
Serves 4.

144

Sweet Chili Eggplant

Sweet Chili Eggplant

Ingredients

5 medium eggplants
½ C white wine vinegar
¾ C chili, deseeded, chopped
½ C olive oil
¼ C liquid sweetener of your choice
3 T salt

Method

Slice the eggplants in 1 cm thick slices and salt them. Let it stand for 10 minutes. Rinse off the excess salt.

In a separate pot, boil the vinegar, chili, olive oil and sweetener until sticky. Pour this sauce over the raw, salted eggplant. Bake at 80°C for 10 to 15 minutes until golden and soft. Serve!

Lasts up to 1 week in the fridge in a sealed container.
Serves 6.

* Every summer we have eggplants in the garden. They are very hearty and satisfying. Also known as aubergine or brinjal.

Handcrafted Spelt Pizza

Base Ingredients

1kg spelt flour, stone ground
1 ½ C water
¼ C olive oil
½ packet dry yeast
1 t salt
1 T liquid sweetener of your choice

Method

Mix all of the base ingredients in a mixer or by hand, allow your mixture to rise in a warm place for 3 to 4 hours. Pull off small fist-sized balls of dough and roll them out on a floured surface to make a pizza base about 25 cm wide and ¼ cm thick.
Pre-bake these bases in the oven for 2 minutes. These keep in the fridge in a sealed container for up to a week.

Napoli Sauce Ingredients

1 C tomato puree,
8 fresh tomatoes, peeled and seeded
2 celery stalks
3 medium carrots, peeled
2 medium onions
¼ C olive oil
2 garlic cloves, peeled
Salt to taste
Black pepper to taste
1 T oregano, fresh or dried
1 T basil, fresh or dried

Method

Pulse the sauce ingredients in a food processor until well mixed but slightly chunky. Store in a glass jar in the fridge for up to a week.

To Make Your Pizza

Choose from the following toppings: mushrooms, olives, red pepper, yellow pepper, eggplant strips, etc.

Spread ¾ C Napoli sauce on the pre-baked pizza base. Arrange the toppings and top with vegan cheese (see recipe on page 169).

Bake the pizza in a very hot oven (250°C or more) for about 4 minutes.

Remove the pizza from the oven, place on a board and cut into slices.

Serve with sliced avocado and fresh rocket. Season your pizza with a dash of olive oil, a pinch of ground clove, ground nutmeg and salt.
Serve hot.

Handcrafted Spelt Pizza

Yota's Spinach Pie

Yota's Spinach Pie

Pastry Ingredients

2 C cake flour, stone-ground
¼ C olive oil
1 C warm water
½ t salt

Pastry Method

Mix the pastry ingredients in a bowl and knead to form a dough that is soft but not sticky. Flour a surface and take half of the dough and roll it out with a rolling pin until it is thin and almost see through (1 mm thick). Line the bottom of a baking dish that is 30 cm x 25 cm with 1 tablespoon of olive oil and then lay the thin pastry in the baking dish, covering the sides. Set aside.

Filling Ingredients

8 C spinach, stems removed, chopped
3 large leeks, roughly chopped
1 C spring onions, chopped
¼ C dill, stems removed, roughly chopped
1 large fennel head and leaves, finely chopped
½ C olive oil
Salt to taste
Black pepper to taste

Filling Method

Pan fry spring onions, leeks, dill and fennel with olive oil until soft.
Wash the spinach, remove stems and chop into small pieces.
Massage the raw spinach by hand in a separate bowl until it is soft and watery.

Toss the fried spring onions, dill, fennel, leeks and raw spinach.
Season with salt and pepper.

Place the spinach mixture evenly into the baking tray on top of the thin pastry. Turn the sides of the pastry into the dish, brush the turned in sides with olive oil and cover the dish completely with the remaining pastry, cutting off the excess edges.

Rub the top of the pastry with olive oil. Score portions lightly with a knife.

Bake for 45 minutes at 200°C or until golden.
Lasts 4 days in the fridge.
Serves 12.

Melanzane Bake

Melanzane Bake

8 eggplants, large
½ C spelt flour
½ C olive oil
2 T salt
1 C Napoli sauce (see recipe on page 167)
¾ C basil pesto (see recipe on page 167)
1 C vegan cheese (see recipe on page 169)

Method

Peel the eggplants, slice them into 1cm thick pieces and lay them in a baking dish. Cover the eggplants with the salt and let them stand for an hour, rinse off the excess salt and water.
This process dehydrates the eggplants to make the bake tastier and less watery.
Cover the wet eggplant with the spelt flour and pan-fry them in the hot olive oil until lightly golden.
Place the eggplants on a kitchen towel and dab off the excess oil, set them aside.
In a medium sized baking tray, cover the base with a thin layer of Napoli sauce, then a layer of the fried eggplants, then another layer of Napoli sauce, then a layer of vegan cheese, then a thin layer of basil pesto, and then repeat the layers until all of the eggplant has been used.
Sprinkle vegan cheese on top of the dish and bake in the oven for 8-10 minutes or until golden.
Serve with fresh rocket.
Lasts up to 3 days in the fridge.
Freezes well.
Serves 8.

Dips & Sauces

*I love sauces...
they make any dish totally
delicious...*

Eggplant Babaghanoush

154

Eggplant Babaghanoush

Ingredients

3 eggplants, large
½ C tahini (sesame seed paste)
3 garlic cloves, peeled
½ bunch of parsley (flat leaf is best), stems removed
¼ C lemon juice, fresh
¼ C olive oil
1 T cumin, ground
Salt to taste
White pepper to taste

Method

Process the ingredients until fairly smooth.
Serve with flatbread or on a sandwich.
Lasts a week in the fridge in a glass jar tightly sealed
and covered with olive oil.
Freezes well.

** Don't be shy with the garlic
and lemon juice!*

Cucumber Tzatziki

Ingredients

2 cucumbers, grated
2 T salt
1 C vegan cheese (see recipe on page 169)
½ garlic clove, finely chopped
1 spring onion, finely chopped
½ bunch dill, chopped
1 T liquid sweetener of your choice
4 T olive oil
1 T lemon zest
Cayenne pepper to taste

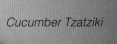

Cucumber Tzatziki

Method

Salt the cucumbers for 10 minutes
and then drain.
Mix the ingredients thoroughly by
hand, in a bowl.
Serve as a dip
   or salad accompaniment.
      Lasts up to 3 days in the fridge.
       Makes 3 cups.

Tomato Salsa

Tomato Salsa

Ingredients

4 tomatoes, medium, firm, chopped
¼ red onion, diced
¼ red chili, seeded, chopped
1 spring onion, chopped
2 T coriander, stems removed
2 T basil, stems removed
2 T red wine vinegar
4 T olive oil
2 garlic cloves
1 cm ginger, peeled and chopped
1 t liquid sweetener of your choice
1 T lemon juice, fresh
White pepper to taste
Salt to taste

Method

Pulse the ingredients in a food processor until chunky or until desired consistency is achieved.
Serve with crackers or chips.
This salsa can also be served on a sandwich.
Lasts up to 5 days in the fridge in a sealed container.
Makes 2 cups.

Salsa Verde

Ingredients

¼ C coriander, fresh
¼ C parsley, fresh
1 T lemon juice, fresh
2 T olive oil
Salt to taste
White pepper to taste

Method

Pulse the ingredients until well combined but not completely smooth.
Lasts up to a week in the fridge.
Makes half a cup.
Freezes well.

Creamy Thyme Dressing

Creamy Thyme Dressing

Ingredients

1/4 C cashews
1 T almond butter, raw
2 T lemon juice, fresh
¾ C water
2 T fresh thyme
1 T dulse flakes
1/4 C olive oil
 Salt to taste

Method

Blend the ingredients on high. Serve on a green salad. Makes one cup. Lasts up to 3 days in the fridge. Freezes well.

Chickpea Hummus

Ingredients

2 C chickpeas, tinned or sprouted
½ C tahini
½ C water or more, as needed
2 garlic cloves, peeled
2 T lemon juice, fresh
1½ t cumin
1 T olive oil
Salt to taste

* Subtitute chickpeas with zucchini for 100% raw hummus.

Method

Blend the ingredients until fairly smooth. Serve with paprika, olive oil and chopped herbs on top.
Makes 2 cups.

Buttery Garlic and Herb Spread

Ingredients

2 C cashews
1 C coconut oil, melted
¼ C olive oil
1 T parsley, chopped
1 t garlic powder
1 garlic clove, peeled
Salt to taste

Method

Blend all the ingredients (except the parsley) on low until incorporated. Pour into a glass container and set in the fridge.
Lasts up to 2 weeks in the fridge.
Freezes well.

Olive Tapenade

Ingredients

1 C olives, de-piped (black or green)
¼ C olive oil
1 T parsley, de-stemmed, chopped
Salt to taste
Pinch white pepper

Method

Process the ingredients until well combined but textured. Lasts up to 3 months in sealed bottles covered with olive oil and kept in the fridge. Freezes well.

Buttery Garlic and Herb Spread

Bruce's Fresh Chili

Ingredients

3 C green chilies, stalks removed
1 C red chilies, stalks removed
5cm ginger, peeled
4 garlic cloves, peeled
2 C basil, de-stemmed
1 C olive oil
Salt to taste
Black pepper to taste

Method

Pulse the ingredients in a food
processor in order to keep the
mixture chunky and textured.
Place in a glass jar for storing
and cover with olive oil.
Lasts up to 3 weeks in the fridge
if well sealed and completely
covered with olive oil.
Freezes well.

Vegan Parmesan

Ingredients

1 C nutritional yeast
¼ C hemp seeds, organic
¼ C sunflower seeds, ground
Salt to taste

Method

Mix the ingredients. Store in a glass
jar in the fridge for up to a month.

Bruce's Fresh Chili

** Nutritional Yeast is extremely high
in Vitamin B12 and has
a very pleasant cheesy taste.*

Vegan Butter

Ingredients

1 C olive oil
1 C coconut oil, melted
½ t turmeric, ground
1 T mixed herbs, dried
Salt to taste

Method

Blend the ingredients on high. Pour in jars and place in the fridge to set. Lasts up to 1 month in the fridge.

Broadbean Pesto

Ingredients

3 C broadbeans, peeled
¼ C lemon juice
2 garlic cloves, peeled
Salt to taste
White pepper to taste

Method

Process the ingredients in a food processor until smooth and creamy. Serve with salad or sandwiches. Lasts up to a week in the fridge if stored in a sealed glass container covered with olive oil.

Vegan Butter

** We have always had broadbeans in the graden.
This is a family favourite.*

Shell's Tofu Mayo

Shell's Tofu Mayo

Ingredients

¼ C plain tofu, cubed
½ C olive oil
1 garlic clove, peeled
¼ C apple cider vinegar
1 t liquid sweetener of your choice
Salt to taste

Method

Blend the ingredients (except tofu). Then add the cubed
tofu slowly until smooth. Lasts up to a week in the fridge.
Freezes well.

Avocado Guacamole

Avocado Guacamole

Ingredients

2 avocados, peeled
½ red onion, finely chopped
1 tomato, finely chopped (optional)
½ bunch coriander, stalks removed, chopped
2 T olive oil
1 t cumin, ground
2 T lemon juice, fresh1 garlic clove, peeled
Red Tabasco to taste or one small red chili (deseeded)
Salt to taste
White pepper to taste

Method

Combine all of the ingredients in a bowl and serve with crackers or chips. Lasts up to 2 days in the fridge.

Napoli Sauce

Napoli Sauce

Ingredients

9 C chopped tinned tomatoes
4 celery stalks, roughly chopped
1 onion, diced
2 carrots, diced
¾ C olive oil
4 garlic cloves, finely chopped
1 T oregano, dried
1 C basil leaves, fresh
1 t liquid sweetener of your choice
White pepper to taste
Salt to taste

Method

Process all the ingredients in a food processor, (except the tomatoes) until finely chopped.
Pan-fry until soft and golden.
Add the tinned tomatoes and bring this mixture to a light boil.
Mix well and remove from heat.
Lasts up to 10 days in the fridge.
Freezes well.
Makes 9 cups of Napoli sauce.

Basil Pesto

Ingredients

1 C basil, fresh, stalks removed
¼ C hemp seeds or cashew nuts
2 T olive oil
1 garlic clove, peeled
1 T lemon juice, fresh
1 T nutritional yeast (optional)
Salt to taste

Method

Place all of the ingredients together in a food processor and process until desired consistency is achieved.
Store in a glass jar in the fridge, covered in olive oil.
Freezes well.
Makes 1 cup.

Vegan Cheese

Vegan Cheese

Ingredients

3 C cashews
2 C water
1 T nutritional yeast
⅛ red onion, peeled
1 garlic clove, peeled
1 t olive oil
1 t lemon juice, fresh
Salt to taste

Method

Blend the ingredients on high until smooth. Pour into jars and place in the fridge.
Lasts up to 5 days in the fridge.
Makes 4 cups of cheese.
Freezes well.

* Add ½ red pepper, any fresh herbs
or chili powder
for variations to this recipe.

Sundried Tomato Pesto

Ingredients

2 C tomatoes, chopped
½ C sundried tomatoes, soaked for
20 minutes in water
2 garlic cloves, peeled
6 basil leaves, stems removed
1½ T olive oil
½ t liquid sweetener of your choice
Salt to taste
White pepper to taste

Method

Pulse the ingredients in a food
processor until chunky. Serve on
sandwiches or a raw pasta dish.
Lasts a week in the fridge in a sealed
container, covered in olive oil.
Makes 2 cups.
Freezes well.

Rocket Mousse

Ingredients

2½ C rocket, fresh
1 C sunflower seeds, soaked for 20
minutes in water
¾ C sesame seeds, soaked for 10
minutes in water
½ C olive oil
½ C water
2 T lemon juice, fresh
3 garlic cloves
Salt to taste

Method

Blend the ingredients on high until
smooth and creamy.
Serve with bread or crackers.
Lasts approximately 5 days
in the fridge.
Freezes well.

* This mousse masks the bitterness
of the rocket. Incorporating the
olive oil last, makes it very creamy.

Mango Salsa

Mango Salsa

Ingredients

2 C mango, diced
3 C tomato, diced
2 red peppers, chopped
½ red onion, finely diced
½ C coriander, stems removed, chopped
1 T chili, ground
2 T lime juice, fresh
Salt to taste
White pepper to taste

Method

Combine the ingredients in a bowl. Serve with chips or crackers or on a salad.
Lasts up to 3 days in the fridge.
Makes 5 cups.

Hall-a-paiñ-o Salsa

Ingredients

6 large tomatoes, red
6 jalapeño peppers
1 large white onion
2 large bunch coriander
3 garlic cloves
Salt to taste

Method

Boil the tomatoes and jalapeños in a pot of water until the tomato skins crack, remove from the water and strain. Place the hot tomatoes and jalapeños in a blender and blend until well broken down and chopped up. Remove from blender and place in a bowl. Chop the onion and garlic very finely and add to the bowl. Chop the coriander slightly more roughly and add to the bowl too. Add salt to taste and mix well.

Serve with corn chips or as an accompaniment to a salad or Mexican dish.

Lasts up to 5 days in the fridge.

Makes 5 cups.

The pointier the peppers, the spicier they are! For a mild salsa, remove all the seeds from the jalapeños.

Snacks

these are great for the drinks table
a fun way to introduce friends
to raw vegan foods...

Caramelized Onions

Caramelized Onions

3 white onions, peeled, thinly sliced
3 T olive oil
2 T tamari (wheat-free soy sauce)
3 T paprika powder

Method

Toss the ingredients in a bowl. Dehydrate at 45°C on a solid sheet for 2 - 3 hours or until soft but fairly dry.
Store in an airtight container in the fridge for up to a week.
Caramelized Onions are wonderful on pizzas, sandwiches and as a topping for salads.

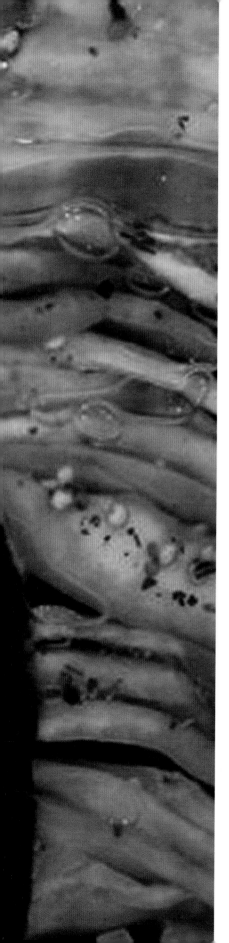

Marinated Eggplant

Ingredients

3 large eggplants, sliced
¼ C bay leaves
1 lemon, thinly sliced
1½ C olive oil
3 garlic cloves, peeled
5 T salt
Black pepper to taste

Method

Place the sliced eggplants in a baking dish and sprinkle it with the salt. This will remove all the excess water. Place something heavy on top of it (like a few covered bricks) and let it dry out overnight. Rinse off the majority of the salt the next day.
Layer the eggplants in a 1 liter glass jar while adding olive oil, a few bay leaves, peeled garlic gloves and pepper to taste.
Cover the top layer with olive oil to preserve.
Lasts up to 3 weeks in the fridge.

To make Eggplant chips

Place these pieces of eggplant in the dehydrator until dry and crispy for approximately 24 hours at 45°C.
Store in a sealed jar or container.

Kale Chips

Kale Chips

4 C kale leaves, washed and stems removed

Dressing Ingredients

1½ C pecans, raw
1 C cashews, raw
2 C water
¼ C lemon juice, fresh
5 T nutritional yeast
3 T apple cider vinegar
1 ¼ C olive oil
3 T miso paste
4 garlic cloves, peeled

Method

Blend the dressing ingredients until very smooth. Massage this dressing onto the kale leaves until they are well coated.

Dehydrate at 50°C for 24 hours or until completely dry.

Lasts up to 3 weeks in an air-tight container.

Makes 4 cups of kale chips.

Onion Bread

Onion Bread

Ingredients

4 medium onions, sliced
1 C sunflower seeds, roughly ground
1 C flaxseeds, ground
½ C tamari (wheat-free soy sauce)
⅓ C olive oil

Method

Mix the ingredients in a bowl, lay the mixture thinly on dehydrator sheets (½ cm thick) and dry at 50°C for approximately 40 hours.
Serve with vegan butter, avocado or a dip of your choice. Lasts up to 2 weeks in a sealed container.
Makes approximately 16 crackers.

Chia Crackers

Chia Crackers

Ingredients

¼ C chia seeds
1½ C water
Salt to taste

Method

Mix the chia seeds, salt and water together until gelatinous.
This should take about 10 minutes.
Optional: add 1 clove finely chopped garlic, 1 T dried herbs
of your choice, or 1 t spices like turmeric or cayenne
pepper.

Dehydrate at 45°C for 2-3 hours or until crispy. This cracker
is light, high in Omega 3 and so easy to make. Lasts up to
2 weeks in a sealed container at room temperature or in the
freezer. Makes 6 - 8 crackers.

Almond Cottage Cheese

Almond Cottage Cheese

Ingredients

1 C almond pulp (left over after making almond milk)
½ red onion, peeled, finely diced
2 chives, finely chopped
¼ C lemon juice, fresh
1 C olive oil
1 C water
1 T mixed herbs, dried
1 t turmeric ground
Salt to taste

Method

Mix the ingredients. Add more lemon juice or water if you find that the cheese is too dry. Lasts up to a week in the fridge. Serve with a salad or cracker.
Makes 1 ½ cups of cheese.

Spicy Nori Sticks

Spicy Nori Sticks

Ingredients

10 nori sheets, unroasted
2 C sunflower seeds, soaked for 20 minutes
2 C carrots, peeled, pureed
½ C parsley, stems removed, chopped
½ C tomato, diced
½ C tamari (wheat-free soy sauce)
1 t cumin powder
2 T lemon juice, fresh
2 T olive oil
2 t curry powder, mild
Black pepper to taste

Method

Blend all the ingredients (except the nori sheets) on high until smooth.
Place a nori sheet flat on a board and add 2 T of this mixture to the one side of your sheet. Spread the mixture in a long line along the one side of the nori sheet. Roll up the sheet. Seal the edges with a drop of water.
Dehydrate the nori sticks at 45°C for 3 to 4 hours or until slightly crispy.
Store them in an airtight container for up to 3 weeks.
Makes 10 nori sticks

Coconut Agave Cashews

Ingredients

1 C cashews, soaked for 30 minutes
⅓ C desiccated coconut
2 T agave

Method

Mix the ingredients well and spread on dehydrator trays in a single layer.
Dehydrate at 45°C for 48 hours or until dry. Store in an airtight container for up to 2 months.
Makes 1 cup of cashews.

Stuffed Peppadews

Ingredients

2 C fresh peppadews
1 C dates, pitted
½ C pomegranate arils, fresh or dried
3 T mesquite powder
Pinch of salt

Method

Clean and deseed the peppadews (wear gloves as they can burn your fingers).
Blend the dates, arils and mesquite on high until smooth.
Stuff each peppadew with this filling and dehydrate at 45°C overnight or until dry.
Lasts up to 2 months in the freezer in a sealed container.

Sweet Coconut Crackers

Sweet Coconut Crackers

Ingredients

4 C fresh coconut meat
2 C carrot juice, fresh
2 T flaxseeds, roughly ground
1 t liquid sweetener of your choice
Pinch salt (optional)

Method

Mix the ingredients in a food processor until fairly smooth.
Spread the mixture thinly onto dehydrator trays (1 cm thick).
Dry at 45°C for approximately 40 hours.
Remove from the trays and cut or break into desired sized crackers. Serve with salad, dip or even gelato (ice cream).
Lasts up to 2 weeks in sealed containers.
Makes approximately 16 crackers.

Moroccan Preserved Lemons

Ingredients

500 g yellow skinned lemons, cut into thin wedges, pips removed
½ C salt
2 garlic cloves, quartered
½ small hot chilies, deseeded, quartered
1 T Allspice
2 bay leaves, roughly torn
Paprika to taste
1 C lemon juice, fresh
½ C olive oil

Method

Dip the lemon wedges in the salt and arrange it in neat layers in a sterilized glass jar. Place the garlic, chilies, allspice and bay leaf between the lemon slices and press down hard.
Pour lemon juice on top.
Pour a layer of olive oil in the top of the jar to seal it. After 3 months, remove the garlic, chilies and bay (at this point they start to get bitter). The lemon lasts up to 3 months in the fridge in sealed containers. Serve with cheese and crackers or curries.

Cheese Sticks

Ingredients

1 C sunflower seeds
1 T lemon juice, fresh
1 TC tamari (wheat-free soy sauce)
1 garlic clove, peeled
½ t mild curry powder
½ t cumin, ground
¼ tomato, chopped
¼ carrot, peeled, chopped
1 T parsley, de-stemmed, chopped
1 t nutritional yeast (optional)

Method

Grind the sunflower seeds in a food processor. Keep ¼ cup of ground seeds aside to roll the cheese sticks in. Blend the remaining ingredients with the ¾ cup of sunflower seeds until the entire mixture is smooth. Place the resulting paste into a pastry piping bag and pipe out thin cheese sticks 3 - 5 cm in length onto a tray. Roll these sticks in the ground seeds. Be gentle as this mixture is very soft. Dehydrate the sticks overnight at 45°C or until dry but not overly crispy. Serve with Napoli sauce (see recipe on page 149). Lovely snack, kids love these too. Lasts up to 3 weeks in a sealed container. Makes 12 cheese sticks.

Can also be served with sundried tomato pesto for a 100% raw snack.

Cheese Sticks

Coconut Bliss Balls

Ingredients

1 ½ C almonds, raw
½ C macadamias, raw
¼ C goji berries
¼ C raisins, soaked for 10 minutes
¼ C coconut flakes
1 T tahini (sesame seed paste)
1 T cashew butter
1 t cinnamon powder
1 t vanilla powder
Pinch salt

Method

Process the ingredients until chunk.
Roll into 2 - 3 cm round balls and cover with desiccated coconut.
Lasts up to a month in the freezer.
Makes 12 balls.

* Use different nuts or seeds, dried fruit and nut butters for variations of this recipe.

Sprouted Wheat Flatbread

Ingredients

1 C wheat kernels, sprouted
¾ onion, chopped
4 T poppy seeds
Salt to taste

Method

Process the wheat kernels in a food processor until doughy.
Add chopped onion and salt.
Process until almost smooth.
Spread thinly on a dehydrator sheet.
Sprinkle the poppy seeds on top of the cracker. Score into squares and dehydrate for 3 hours at 45°C.
Remove from dehydrator, turn and place back in the dehydrator until dry.
Do not over dehydrate.
Serve with vegan butter, hummus or guacamole.
Lasts up to a month in a sealed container.
Makes 8 crackers.

Desserts

All our desserts are lactose free
and mostly wheat & gluten free...
suitable for almost everyone to enjoy...

Kotze's Florentines

Kotze's Florentines

Ingredients

1½ C hulled buckwheat, sprouted*
1 C sunflower seeds
1 C cacao paste, melted
1 C cacao butter, melted
½ C liquid sweetener of your choice
1 C raisins
2 vanilla pods, scraped
1 C goji berries
½ C dried fruit (cranberries, apricots, peaches, etc.), chopped
½ C pumpkin seeds
Salt to taste

Method

Mix the ingredients in a bowl. Shape the mixture into even sized balls. Roll and flatten into thick patties about 2 cm thick and 6 cm wide.
Place in the fridge to set on a non-stick tray.
Lasts up to 2 weeks in the freezer.
Makes approximately 20 florentines.

*You can buy already sprouted
and hulled buckwheat from most health stores,
or you can soak it overnight in water, rinse well the next
day and then dehydrate at 45°C overnight to dry.

Mixed Berry Crumble

Base Ingredients

3 C cashews, raw
4 T liquid sweetener of your choice
1 T coconut oil, melted
Salt to taste

Base Method

Blend the base ingredients until smooth and press firmly into the bottom of a medium sized baking tray about 2 cm thick.

Filling Ingredients

3 C frozen berries of your choice
½ C liquid sweetener of your choice
¼ C fresh young coconut meat
1 T lemon juice, fresh
¼ vanilla pod, scraped
Salt to taste

Filling Method

Blend the filling ingredients until fairly smooth. Place on top of base in a baking tray and set in the freezer.

Crumble Topping Ingredients

1 C pecans, raw
½ C cashews, raw
¼ C liquid sweetener of your choice
2 T coconut oil, melted
1 t cinnamon powder
¼ vanilla pod, scraped
Salt to taste

Topping Method

Pulse the topping ingredients in a food processor until crumbly. Add some of the crumble to the top of the dish.
Place back in the freezer to set.

Glaze Ingredients

½ C cashews, raw
½ C young coconut meat
¼ C liquid sweetener of your choice
¼ C water
3 T coconut oil, melted
1 t vanilla extract
Salt to taste

Glaze Method

Pulse the glaze ingredients in a food processor until smooth. Add some of the glaze to the top of the dish.
Place back in the freezer to set.
Lasts up to 2 weeks in the freezer.
Serves 14.

Mixed Berry Crumble

Chocolate Tart

Chocolate Tart

Base Ingredients

1 C almonds, soaked for 1 hour in water
1 C cashews, soaked for 30 minutes in water
½ C cacao powder, raw
¼ C flaxseeds, ground *
¼ C liquid sweetener of your choice *Ground flaxseeds are a great binder.
¼ C maple syrup Other binders are coconut oil, avocado,
Pinch of salt buckwheat flour, chia gel
and irish moss paste.

Base Method

Process the ingredients until fairly smooth.
Press this base into the bottom of a medium sized tart pan.
Set in the freezer.

Filling Ingredients

2 C cashews, soaked for 30 minutes in water
½ C liquid sweetener of your choice
½ C cacao powder, raw
½ C water For variations add coarse salt,
½ C coconut oil, melted cayenne pepper or ground coffee
Pinch of salt to garnish the chocolate tart.

Filling Method

Blend the filling ingredients until very smooth.
Pour into the base and freeze to set.
Lasts up to 2 weeks in the freezer.
Serves 16.

Chocolate Orange Cheesecake

Base Ingredients

½ C cashews, raw
½ C pecans, raw
1 T coconut oil, melted
2 T cacao powder, raw
2 T liquid sweetener of your choice
1 T lemon juice, fresh

Base Method

Process the base ingredient until fairly smooth. Push this mixture into the bottom of a 20 cm round cake dish and set in the freezer.

First Layer Ingredients

1 C cashews, soaked for 30 minutes
¾ C cacao butter, melted
¼ C liquid sweetener of your choice
⅓ C orange juice, fresh
1 T orange zest
½ vanilla pod, scraped

First Layer Method

Blend the first layer ingredients on high until very smooth and pour on top of base. Set in the freezer.

Second Layer Ingredients

1 C cashews, soaked for 30 minutes
⅓ C cacao powder, raw
¾ C cacao butter, melted
⅓ C liquid sweetener of your choice
⅓ C orange juice, fresh
½ vanilla pod, scraped

Second Layer Method

Blend the second layer ingredients on high until very smooth. Pour on top of the first layer. Set in the freezer.
Lasts up to 2 weeks in the freezer.
Serves 16.

Serve with a sprinkle of cacao powder and a slice fresh orange.

Chocolate Orange Cheesecake

Kotze's Pear Pudding

Ingredients

4 pears, diced
1 vanilla pod, scraped
1 t nutmeg, ground
1 t cinnamon powder

Method

Mix all ingredients in a bowl. Place into a baking dish that is at least 4 cm deep.

Vanilla Sauce

½ C coconut water
½ C cashews, soaked for
30 minutes
½ C macadamias, soaked for
30 minutes
1 vanilla pod, scraped
¼ C liquid sweetener of your choice
Pinch of salt

Sauce Method

Blend on high until smooth. Place 4 tablespoons on top of the pear mixture in the baking dish.

Crunchy Topping Ingredients

2 C pecans, chopped
1 C liquid sweetener of your choice
½ t cinnamon powder
½ vanilla pod, scraped
Pinch of salt

Topping Method

Process the topping ingredients until chunky but well mixed. Sprinkle this topping onto the pear mixture and place dish in the freezer to set.
Lasts up to 3 days in the fridge.
Serves 3.

Goji Berry Bar

Ingredients

1 C goji berries
½ C coconut oil, melted
½ C cashews, raw
½ C dates, pitted
½ C cranberries, dried
1 vanilla pod, scraped
¼ C cacao nibs, raw

Method

Process the ingredients in a food processor until the mixture binds well. Place mixture in a baking dish about 3 cm thick, pushing it down evenly. Place in fridge and let it set.
Slice into even sized bars.
Keeps in the fridge for up to 2 weeks.
Makes approximately 14 small bars.

Goji Berry Bar

Raw Chocolate Truffles

Raw Chocolate Truffles

Ingredients

¾ C cacao powder, raw
1 ½ C cashew butter
¾ C liquid sweetener of your choice
1 vanilla pod, scraped
1 t cinnamon powder
¾ C cacao butter, melted
Salt to taste

Method

Blend the ingredients on high until very smooth. Divide into even sized portions. Roll in cacao nibs or your choice from the following: hemp seeds, desiccated coconut, chopped nuts, chopped goji berries, cinnamon, etc. Lasts in the fridge for up to 3 weeks. Makes approximately 15 truffles.

Orange Toffee

Ingredients

1 C hazelnuts, raw
1 C cacao powder, raw
½ C coconut oil, melted
½ C cacao butter, melted
1 C liquid sweetener of your choice
2 t vanilla extract
8 t orange zest, fresh
Pinch of salt

Method

Blend the ingredients until well
incorporated and smooth.
Place mixture about 3 cm high
in a non-stick baking tray.
Set in the freezer overnight.
Cut into 5 cm pieces.
Lasts up to 3 weeks in the freezer.
Makes 18 toffees.

Homemade Chocolates

Ingredients

2 C cacao paste, raw
1 C cacao butter, raw
½ C liquid sweetener of your choice
1 vanilla pod, scraped
Salt to taste

Method

Melt the cacao paste and cacao butter
until it reaches approximately 60°C.
Blend it on low in a blender. Slowly add
sweetener to taste, vanilla and salt.
Pour into chocolate moulds.
Add variations to your taste:
1 T of ground coffee, goji berries, hemp
seeds, any superfood powders, nuts,
seeds, orange zest, etc.
Lasts up to 3 weeks in the fridge
Freezes well.
Makes up to 30 chocolates.

Homemade Chocolates

Chocolate Nut Milk

Ingredients

1 C nut milk of your choice (almond or cashew are best*)
2 T cacao powder, raw
2 T cashews, raw
3 pitted dates
½ vanilla pod, scraped
½ t cinnamon powder
1 C ice

Method

Blend the ingredients on high. Serve chilled.
Lasts up to 2 days in the fridge in a sealed jar.
Serves 2.

*To make nut milk:
blend 1 cup of nuts
with 3 cups of water
and strain through a nut milk bag.

Raw Apple Pie

Crust Ingredients

1½ C macadamias, raw
½ C almonds, raw
1 C dates, pitted
½ C water
Pinch of salt

Crust Method

Process the crust ingredients in a food processor until fairly smooth. Press into a tart pan, forming a ½ cm crust.

Filling Ingredients

3 C apples, finely chopped
3 T lemon juice
4 T cashew butter
¼ C liquid sweetener of your choice
1 T cinnamon
¼ t nutmeg
One vanilla pod, scraped

Filling Method

Mix the filling ingredients.
Once the crust is set, fill the crust with the filling.
Stores in the freezer for up to 2 weeks.
Serves up to 16.

Raw Apple Pie

213

Chia Parfait

Ingredients

4 T chia seeds
1 C water
2 T cashews, raw
2 T liquid sweetener of your choice
1 T cacao powder, raw
Cinnamon powder to taste
¼ t nutmeg, ground
¼ t ginger, fresh, grated
¼ vanilla pod, scraped
Salt to taste
¼ banana

Method

Soak the chia seeds in water, mix well and let it stand for 5 minutes, stir until all lumps have been removed.
Blend the remaining ingredients on high until smooth. Then mix with the chia "gel". Serve in a small glass, top with chopped banana. Lasts up to 2 days in the fridge.

Chia Parfait

Chocolate Macadamia Rocky Road

Chocolate Macadamia Rocky Road

Ingredients

2½ C cacao paste, melted
2 C cacao butter, melted
½ C liquid sweetener of your choice
1 vanilla pod, scraped
1½ C macadamias, chopped
Pinch of salt

Method

Mix the ingredients in a large bowl while it's still liquid. Pour the mixture into a non-stick baking dish and set in the freezer.
Break or slice into log shapes.
Lasts up to 3 weeks in the fridge (covered).
Makes 20 logs.

Natalie's Pancakes

Ingredients

3 C coconut butter (made from blended coconut flakes)
3 C oat flour
3 bananas
1 C dried mango or dried apple
3 T coconut blossom sugar
2 T mesquite powder (white carob)
1 T lucuma powder
1 T cinnamon powder
½ C almonds, raw
2 T coconut oil, melted
1 vanilla pod, scraped
1 C almond milk, fresh
1 T lemon juice, fresh
2 T buckwheat flour

Method

Process the coconut butter, oat flour, bananas and dried fruit in a food processor.
Add the rest of the ingredients and process until well combined.
Pre-heat the oven to 170 °C.
Prepare an oven tray by lightly rubbing it with coconut oil.
Drop a tablespoon of the pancake mix onto the tray and shape it with the back of a spoon into your desired pancake size (10 cm round).
Bake the pancakes until the bottom edges start to go brown.
Flip the pancakes and bake until brown. This takes about 10 minutes on each side.
Serve with vanilla gelato, strawberries and desiccated coconut.
Lasts up to 5 days in the fridge.
Makes 15 pancakes.

Raw Gelato

Raw Gelato

All of our gelatos (ice creams)
are dairy free and free of
refined sugars but truly
delicious and creamy.

Ingredients

1 C cashews, soaked for 30 minutes
1 C fresh young coconut meat
¼ C liquid sweetener of your choice
1 C almond milk, fresh
½ vanilla pod, scraped
Pinch salt

Method

Blend the ingredients on high until very smooth.

For variations you can add strawberries, goji berries, cacao powder, coffee, cinnamon, any other fruit, mint, etc and blend again.

Pour the mixture into an ice cream machine and mix.
Store in a container in the freezer.
Lasts up to 3 weeks in the freezer.
Makes 10 scoops.

Goji Berry Cheesecake

Crust Ingredients

1 C almonds, raw
1 C cashews, raw
½ C hemp seeds
½ vanilla pod, scraped
1 t salt
3 T liquid sweetener of your choice

Crust Method

Process the crust ingredients until well combined and crusty. Push the crust mix into a cake mould and set in the freezer.

Filling Ingredients

5 C cashews, soaked in water for 1 hour
½ vanilla pod, scraped
3 T lecithin powder
¾ C xylitol, blended until fine like icing sugar
2 C almond milk, fresh
¾ C coconut oil, melted
1 C lemon juice, fresh
¼ t salt
1 C water
1 C goji berries, soaked for 10 minutes
1 T mesquite powder
1 T maca powder
1 T lucuma powder

Filling Method

Blend the filling ingredients, except the coconut oil. Blend on high until very smooth. Add the coconut oil last and continue to blend until smooth. Pour the filling into the cake mould on top of the base and set in the freezer.
Decorate with coconut flakes and goji berries. To create a beautiful pattern, sprinkle a few drops of freshly squeezed beetroot juice onto the cake and swirl it around with a spoon.

*Soaking the cashews allows them to soften so they can be extra smooth and creamy for the filling of the cake.

*Mesquite is an excellent source of manganese, zinc, calcium, potassium, iron, lysine and soluble fiber. It has a caramel-like taste and is derived from the carob tree. It is low on the glycaemic index and has a naturally sweet taste. It grows well in Southern Africa.

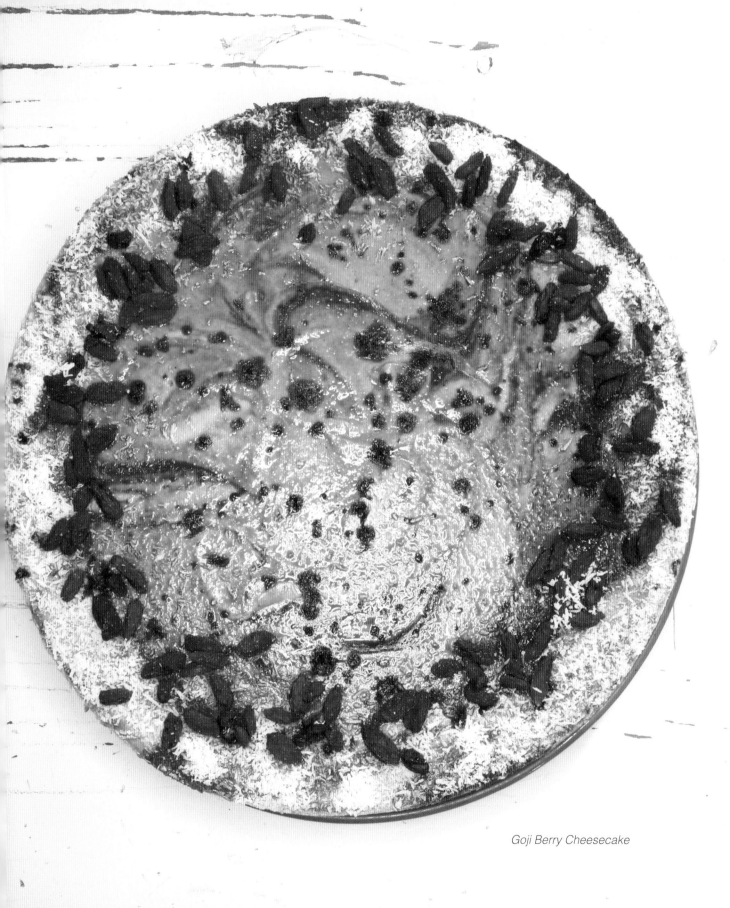

Goji Berry Cheesecake

This is one of Leafy Greens Café's most famous dishes!

Strawberry Cheesecake

Strawberry Cheesecake

Base Ingredients

1 C almonds, raw
1 C cashews, raw
2 vanilla pods, scraped
3 T liquid sweetener of your choice
1 T coconut oil, melted
1 t salt

Base Method

Process the ingredients for the base in a food processor until fairly smooth.
Press into the bottom of a spring form cake tin about 1 - 2 cm thick. Set in the freezer.

First Layer Ingredients

3 C cashews, soaked for 30 minutes
¾ C liquid sweetener of your choice
1/2 C coconut oil, melted
1½ C almond milk, fresh
1 C lemon juice
3 T lecithin powder
¼ t salt

First Layer Method

Blend the first layer ingredients on high until perfectly smooth. Pour half of this mixture on top of the base into the spring form cake tin.

For **the second layer**, blend the other half of the mixture with 5 large strawberries. Pour on top of the first layer and set in the freezer.
Lasts 2 weeks in the freezer and a week in the fridge.
Serves 16.

Coconut Tart

Base Ingredients

2 C coconut flakes
¼ C coconut butter
1 date, pitted
¼ t vanilla essence
¼ C water
Pinch of salt

Base Method

Process the base ingredients in the food processor until well combined and a dough-like consistency is reached. Press this dough into a tart pan. Set in the freezer.

Filling Ingredients

2 C coconut water
½ C coconut oil, melted
¾ C fresh young coconut meat
½ C dates, pitted
½ C water
1 T vanilla essence
2 T lecithin granules
Pinch of salt

Filling Method

Blend the filling ingredients on high until extremely smooth. Pour onto the base. Set in the freezer.
Serve this tart sprinkled with desiccated coconut and a few blueberries on the side.
Serves 14.

Coconut Tart

Carrot Cake

Cake Ingredients

2 ¼ C gluten free flour
1 t baking powder
1 ¼ t baking soda
½ t salt
2 t cinnamon, ground
½ t nutmeg, ground
½ t ginger, ground
¼ C flaxseeds, ground
¾ C warm water
1 ¼ C xylitol
1 C olive oil
2 t vanilla extract
Zest of one orange
¼ C orange juice, fresh
3 C carrots, peeled and grated
1 ½ C walnuts, chopped
½ C vegan butter (see recipe on page 143)

Cake Method

Preheat the oven to 180°C.
Mix the cake ingredients untill well combined.
Pour into a cake tin.
Bake for 40 minutes. Check if the cake is cooked through by pricking it.
Let the cake cool for 2 hours before icing.

Raw Icing Ingredients

1 C cashews, raw
1 C water
½ C macadamias, raw
4 T lemon juice, fresh
1 vanilla pod, scraped
2 T olive oil
1 T liquid sweetener of your choice
1 t lecithin granules
Pinch of salt

Icing Method

Blend the icing ingredients. Pipe the icing onto the cake in patterns.
Garnish with cinnamon.
Serves 18.

Banana Cream Pie

Crust Ingredients

1 ½ C macadamias, raw
½ C coconut flakes
½ t salt
3 T liquid sweetener of your choice
1 T coconut oil, melted
1 t vanilla extract

Banana Cream Filling Ingredients

3 C soaked cashews
2 C mashed banana
1 C liquid sweetener of your choice
2 t vanilla extract
1 T lemon juice, fresh
¼ t salt
½ C coconut oil, melted

Coconut Cream Ingredients

1 ½ C cashews, soaked for one hour in water
1 ½ C coconut milk
½ C liquid sweetener of your choice
1 T vanilla extract
1 t lemon juice, fresh
1 C coconut oil, melted
Pinch of salt
1 sliced banana for layering

Method

To make the crust place the macadamia nuts, shredded coconut and salt in a food processor and process until crumbly. Add sweetener, coconut oil, and vanilla; lightly pulse until all ingredients are well mixed but only stick together when pressed between the fingers.

To make the banana cream filling, blend all the ingredients except the coconut oil in a high speed blender until smooth. Add the coconut oil and blend until combined.

To make the coconut cream, blend the first five ingredients in a blender until smooth. Then add coconut oil and salt and continue to blend until completely combined. Put in the refrigerator for a few minutes so it can set.

To assemble, press crust into a 20 cm tart pan with a removable bottom. Pour in banana cream filling. Top with banana slices. Top with coconut cream. Let set in the fridge for at least 30 minutes before serving.

Cecilia's Fruit Bread

Ingredients

1 C gluten-free oats
1 C buckwheat flour
½ C almond pulp (left over from making almond milk)
1/3 C sunflower seeds
1/3 C pumpkin seeds
2 T chia seeds
1 T gluten free flour
1 T coconut oil, melted
2 t bicarbonate of soda
Pinch of salt
2 T cinnamon powder
½ C almond milk
1 apple, grated
2 bananas, peeled, mashed
¼ C dried apricots or dried apples
½ C liquid sweetener of your choice

Method

Mix all of the ingredients together until well combined, kneed the mixture for another few minutes. Bake the loaf in the oven at 200°C for 40 minutes in a medium-sized baking dish, then check the loaf and bake for a further 10 minutes as needed or until golden and baked through.

Testimonials

Michele Throssell's Story

For as long as I can remember, healthy food has always been part of our daily lives. So much so, that we almost took it for granted! We grew a lot of our own vegetables and fruit and were regulars at the local farm stalls and home industries. Free-range chicken and organic vegetables were the norm. When visiting friends' homes, I was always amazed to see white sugar, white bread, processed cereals and Coke. For me, it was unheard of!

Just over a year ago, I was diagnosed with breast cancer. It was a shock to both myself and my family and friends. I had so many questions. Where did it come from? Why me? Why is this tumour growing in my body? I knew I was destined to learn something from this.

The initial phase was frightening. I felt incredibly pressurised to follow the doctor's advice, but after 6 weeks of considering my options and with the support of all of my family, I decided that, after the mastectomy, I would follow the natural route of healing my mind, body and soul.

I visited Hippocrates Health Institute in the USA. They helped and guided me into the natural healing process. Up to that point, I had already been eating extremely healthy foods and I knew that I needed to support my body physically to get rid of any toxins and degenerative cells. Hence, I decided to boost my diet by eating 100% raw, living foods, drinking lots of green juices and taking wheatgrass shots twice a day. I added enzymes and probiotics to my diet and increased my intake of minerals, plant-based omega oils, B12, iodine, multi-vitamins and minerals. I added massages, colonic irrigation to keep my colon clean, as well as intravenous oxygen, ozone treatments, vitamin C and immune boosters to my treatment. That was the physical side, but I knew work had to be done on discovering what was emotionally stored in the tumour.

I realised that, with breast cancer, we need to release the fear and know that the intelligence of the universe resides in each one of us. We are normally very self-critical. Learning to love and accept ourselves, together with the right diet and meditation, are the keys to healing cancer. This was the route I chose to follow.

Once we learn what the physical block to our health is, and we finally let go of the emotional issues stored in the cells, then, and only then, can real healing begin at all levels - emotionally, physically and spiritually. The body then goes through the process of healing itself naturally. I knew my journey would have to include letting go of whatever emotional issues were being held inside the cancer tumour.

It took quite a long time to discover what those issues were. I feel stronger every day, and feel truly blessed to have found this natural way of healing.

Accepting my fate and the journey that follows, is something that I am incredibly grateful for. I have grown spiritually, physically and mentally and realised, after embarking on this mind-body venture, that everything happens for a reason and a purpose.

Considering the world's focus on convenience foods and the demanding pace of life, I am so proud of Antonia and her decision to follow such a wonderfully healthy lifestyle, She has studied and been passionate about her choices and has a beautiful spirit to complement it. Well done, my dear, special niece - may your book be appreciated and loved by everyone who reads it!

Michele Throssell

Cosimo's story

My mom and I volunteered at a home for abandoned babies called Acres of Love. We bathed, fed and played with the children who had been found on street corners and in abusive homes. One day, my mom met a little boy called Nkosi Zulu. Nkosi's mother was an alcoholic and so he was born with foetal alcohol syndrome and terrible eczema. He was one year old when we met him. He was not doing well at the home and my mother was desperate to help. She asked my father if we could bring Nkosi home with us for 3 months to get him well again. I still remember that first day that we had Nkosi: his little body so covered with sores from all the alcohol and he stank so badly, my father had to wear a mask. We coated his body in flaxseed oil and wrapped him in bandages. With the help of the flaxseed oil, a clean diet and sunlight in the early morning, his eczema started to heal. It was so sad to see this little innocent child, bearing the consequences of his mother's actions. But every day he grew stronger and healthier. We fed him a simple fruit and vegetable diet consisting mainly of avocado, banana, paw paw and dates. We massaged his slightly deformed feet until they grew straighter. Cosi began to get well. (Cosi was the name of my father's great grandfather and so we began to call him this.) Needless to say, he stayed much longer than 3 months and he is still with us today. Cosi is now the most perfect child. We are very blessed.

Antonia De Luca

Aunty Wilma's Story

From a young age I had problems with my stomach. In the prime of my life, I had to undergo various stomach operations, and each time part of my stomach was removed.

At the age of 69, I was told I would have to have what was left of my stomach totally removed. I decided not to have this operation and was inspired and assisted by my wonderful niece Jennifer to rather go onto a 100 % raw food diet. I did this for two and a half years - for which I am extremely grateful. I am so blessed that I am well and healthy and I now realise just how fortunate I was to be introduced to this way of life and to take charge of my health and well-being.

Wilma Jacobs.

Academy & Workshops.

Every second month we host a full-day raw food chef's academy at the conference centre at Leafy Greens. It's a hands-on, gourmet, raw food and vegan chef training and we are completely open with regards to the recipes that participants would like to learn. The course includes the use of a chef's jacket for the day, a Leafy Greens apron, all the food for the day, a certificate and a large recipe file.

We also offer private academies for a minimum of 6 people, an introduction to raw food course, raw chocolate making courses, and many more.

Our cooked vegan workshops include Mediterranean, Moroccan, Indian, Chinese and World Cuisine.

Apart from our culinary workshops, our conference centre has been home to numerous book launches, author days as well as external training and learning courses. Our tranquil setting and magnificent gardens have also inspired our Yoga Wellness Days.

Please keep us in mind for your next training course, function, launch or event.
E-mail mytable@leafygreens.co.za to book or find out more on our website www.leafygreens.co.za

Facebook www.facebook.com/lgcafe. Instagram: @leafygreenscafe. Twitter: @leafygreenscafe

"Let food be thy medicine
and medicine be thy food" Hippocrates

Glossary

Sprouting. Sprouts are so easy to grow and they have unlimited health benefits. Sprouts contain protein, iron, vitamins, minerals, enzymes and are alkaline-forming. The variety of sprouts include fenugreek, wheat, alfalfa, mung bean, adzuki bean, green peas, sunflowers, beetroot, broccoli, mustard and many more. The seeds are soaked in water overnight and rinsed twice a day thereafter until a little sprout forms. At this stage it is ready to eat or plant. Wheat, pea greens and sunflower sprouts are planted in potting soil so that the micro-greens can be harvested and enjoyed.

Superfoods. Nutrient-rich foods considered being especially beneficial for health and well-being. They contain the highest nutrients of any other respective food. Goji berries are extremely high in anti-oxidants and is a good example of a superfood.

Fermented (cultured) foods. Fermentation is the conversion of carbohydrates to organic acids using living bacteria under anaerobic conditions. The term "fermentation" is sometimes used to refer to the chemical conversion of sugars into ethanol, a process that is used to produce alcoholic beverages. Examples of fermented or cultured foods are kim chi, sauerkraut, kefir, kombucha, vinegar, wine and beer. Fermented foods balance the flora in the gut and aid digestion.

Nut milks. One cup of nuts or seeds to three cups of water, blended on high and strained through a nut milk bag. Any nuts or seeds can be used: almonds, cashews, macadamias, pecans, walnuts, hazelnuts, hemp seeds, sunflower seeds, pumpkin seeds, sesame seeds, etc. The left over pulp can be used to make nut cottage cheese or it can be dehydrated and grounded into flour. This flour is gluten and wheat free.

Wheatgrass. Organic wheat kernels can be used to grow wheatgrass. The seeds are soaked in water overnight and then placed in a sprouting container or a jar and rinsed twice daily until a sprout is formed. This takes up to 3 days. Once sprouted, plant the seeds in a tray filled with organic potting soil that has drainage holes in the bottom. Cover the sprouts with another tray in order for them to germinate in the dark. Remove the lid after one day. When the wheatgrass has grown to approximately 10 cm high cut and juice within 5 days.

Soaking. Soaking nuts or seeds in water helps to release the enzyme inhibitors that some varieties contain. Discard the water after soaking and rinse the nuts before use. Harder nuts like almonds can be soaked overnight. Softer nuts like cashews and pecans should only be soaked for 1 - 2 hours.

Food combining. Combining proteins, starches, fats and fruits correctly in the diet helps the body to digest food easier and assists in the absorption of vitamins and minerals. Proteins and starches should be eaten separately but both can be combined with vegetables. Acid, sub-acid and sweet fruits should also be eaten separately. Melons should be eaten alone. (See Mary-Ann Shearer's Food Combining Guide for more info).

Spiralizing. A spiralizer is a fun and easy hand operated vegetable slicer that can be used to create different cuts in fruits and vegetables. The finest 0.9 mm angel hair attachment can be used to make fine spaghettis. The thickness of the blades vary in size. It also shreds, slices and flutes vegetables and fruit. This machine is great for children to use.

Sweeteners. Honey, xylitol, maple syrup, coconut sugar.

Blending. A high-speed blender (e.g. Vitamix) makes raw food very easy to prepare. It blends dates, ice and nuts with ease. It makes making nut butters, smoothies, cakes and soups easy.

Food processing. A Magimix or a Robot Coupe Food Processor can be used to make dishes such as pestos, hummus and other dips and cracker bases. It allows some texture to remain in the dish.

Genetically Modified Foods. These are foods grown or made from organisms that have had specific changes made to its DNA, using methods of genetic engineering. These techniques have allowed the introduction of new crops, as well as greater control over a food's genetic structure: the way it grows, the speed it grows at, etc. GM foods have a negative effect on the body and the DNA. GM foods are not recommended for human consumption.

Organics. Organics are foods that are produced using methods of organic farming, without the use of synthetic pesticides and chemical fertilizers. Organic foods are also generally not subjected to radiation, industrial solvents, or chemical additives. It is higher in vitamins and minerals.

Coconut oil. Coconut oil is anti-fungal, anti-viral and anti-microbial. It stays stable at very high temperatures, therefore it is the best oil for frying. Coconut oil can also be used on the body as a moisturizer. It has many benefits and uses.

Seaweeds. Seaweed is extremely high in iodine and iron, they are found on most coastlines around the world. The most popular varieties are dulse, kelp, nori, wakame, hijiki and sea lettuce. It is high in fiber and mostly a complete protein. It can be added to salads, soups, cooked dishes and sushi dishes.

Dehydrating. Dehydrating is drying at low temperatures to retain enzymes. The general temperature at which enzymes denature is 45°C. It is a very useful tool to preserve food. It removes the water from the produce and allows it to last longer. Cookies, dried fruit, crackers, wraps, pizza bases, bliss balls and lots more can be made using a dehydrator. If a dehydrator is not available, an oven can be used on low with a spoon in the door to keep it ajar and allow the moisture to evaporate.

Nut flours. These flours are made from the left over pulp after making nut milk. The pulp is dehydrated at a low temperature and blended into flour. Almond, cashew, pecan or any other nuts make lovely nut flours that are great for baking.

Measurements
Capital 'T' = tablespoon. 1 tablespoon = 15ml
Small 't' = teaspoon. 1 teaspoon = 5ml
Capital 'C' = cup. 1 cup = 250ml,   ½ cup = 125ml

Gluten and wheat intolerance. Many people who suffer from these intolerances, are unaware of it and live with the symptoms. Wheat can result in bloating, itching, Candida, excess mucus, and eczema. Gluten can result in colon blockages, diarrhea, poor absorption of minerals, iron deficiencies, etc. Wheat and gluten are found in all wheat products and commercial flours, cakes, muffins, pastries, oats, rye and barley. Gluten and wheat free grains include quinoa, millet, buckwheat, amaranth and teff.

Index

My notes

Recommended Equipment

Juicer: A slow, masticating juicer is the best juicer as it uses a very gentle process to extract juice from your fruits and vegetables and therefore the enzymes stay alive and the juice lasts longer (up to 3 days in the fridge in a sealed container). This type of "screw" juicer is able to juice wheatgrass, sprouts and greens.

Centrifugal juicers that use spinning and sieving methods cannot extract juice from leafy greens, sprouts and wheatgrass.

High-speed Blender: The Vitamix is a blender in a class of its own. It chops nuts and coconut, blends smoothies silky smooth, purées and makes cream dips and sauces. It can also blend juices of your choice. If you take care of this machine, you will have it for life.

Food Processor: Magimix or Robot Coupe are very good food processor brands.
A food processor helps to achieve a chunky but well mixed consistency.
Perfect for making cake crusts, pestos, hummus, raw pizza bases and crackers.